Love and Forgiveness
A New Way to Live

The principles presented in this book provide

a life-altering experience —

regardless of one's religious beliefs.

Love and Forgiveness

A New Way to Live

by Lorene McClintock

Love and Forgiveness: A New Way to Live
by Lorene McClintock

Library of Congress Control Number 2004: 2004108167

Published in the United States by
McClintock Enterprises, 2004

First U.S. printing, 2004

ISBN: 1-880556-61-8

Printed in the United States on acid-free paper

Book and cover design by Maida Landau
Production and printing by Mel Byrd, Ink.

Distributed by McClintock Enterprises
853 Seventh Avenue, New York, NY 10019

For information, contact:
McClintock Enterprises
853 Seventh Avenue, New York, NY 10019

www.lorenemcclintock.com

Contents

Table of Contents

Table of Contents

Table of Contents

Acknowledgments

To acknowledge my appreciation and gratitude to all of you who have read the manuscript of this book would be an impossible task.

Your deeply moving accounts of how your lives have been transformed through practicing the principles as they are presented in this work have provided the assurance, encouragement, and support that I needed to be able to trust my inspiration, and to confidently undertake to explain and clarify particular spiritual subjects in a way that I have not encountered elsewhere.

Your enthusiastic and loving response and your constant urging me to "hurry up" and release this work for publication have brought me to this point. And so, here is the book.

My most heartfelt thanks to each one of you.

Lovingly,

Preface

This book contains spiritual principles that are Universal. There is only one Truth, but there are many interpretations and many religions.

I found in the Bible and in the works of Joel S. Goldsmith the spiritual principles and quotations that form the basis of this book. If you follow a different religious belief, you may not be familiar with the particular quotations that I have used. But you may find the same or similar principles in your own religious scripture and writings.

The purpose of this book, *Love and Forgiveness: A New Way to Live,* is to present a way that will enable all of us to practice the principles of living spiritually.

My Story
A Summary

Read this first

—————— My Story: A Summary ——————

What I'm going to tell you now may not seem to have anything to do with *Love and Forgiveness: A New Way to Live.* But my purpose in telling you this is to give you the beginning of my story, and to provide a background for the development of what is to come.

I grew up in a small town in Texas. I was an only child, and every Sunday I went to church with my parents. The first activity each Sunday morning was Sunday School, where I learned Bible stories with other children. And after Sunday School, I went to the regular church service with the grown-ups. I have no recollection, however, of any spiritual inspiration that I took home with me on Sundays. Going to church was just something we did.

I was not taught to kneel down and say a prayer before I went to bed at night. But when I got into bed, I pulled the covers up over my head and talked to God. I always felt as if I didn't belong, and that nobody really understood me. I wanted to be understood and to understand. And when I talked to God, I felt secure and comforted. This was a secret I never shared with anyone.

In the small town where we lived, I was one of a privileged few who took piano lessons, and one of an even smaller number who went on to study music in college. I began piano lessons at the age of seven. And every year, until I finished high school, I played in a music festival or a contest — always winning a blue ribbon or a gold medal. From the time I was a senior in high school until I went away to college, I played the piano for the Sunday services at the church — rehearsing with the choir one night during the week.

Although the study of music took precedence, I was — even as a small child — interested in painting and fashion design. During my first year in college, I studied art as well as music, carrying notes back and forth between my art teacher and my music teacher, each telling the other that my talent lay in their particular field, and that I needed more time to devote to their assignments. There was no question, however, that music would win — and so it did.

Throughout my college years, my piano teachers spoke of my talent as exceptional, and when I graduated, they urged me to consider a career as a performer. Although I did give some concerts, I certainly had no intention of pursuing such a career.

I wanted to teach. I didn't know exactly why or how, but there was something within me that knew that there was a deeper meaning to music than I had — up to that point — discovered. And so, without a formalized system, I began to teach piano.

My first students were children, but before long, I found that almost every adult I met said to me, "I've always wanted to play the piano." So I began to teach adult beginners, individually, and later, in groups.

I was always interested in challenges. I knew that in order for the students to learn to read music and play the piano, they shouldn't look at the keys. And so, to enable them to establish coordination between the eyes and the hands, I developed what I called a "signal-and-response system." And then, I invented and patented a Keyboard Concealer and Interval Keyblocks, which are described later in the book.

I devised a method, using only one piano, to teach large groups of students. And I taught at several institutions and universities. In hospitals, without using a piano, I taught patients with mental and physical disabilities — including bed patients. All this time, I was developing a totally new approach to teaching the piano. Later, I trained teachers who wished to use the method I had devised.

Intermittently, I would digress from teaching music and be carried away with some ideas about fashion design or painting — always receiving such positive response that I was tempted to go off in a whole new direction. But once, upon observing my dilemma, a man asked me, "What do you want to do more than anything else?" I couldn't make a decision on that basis, because I wanted to paint, I wanted to design, and I wanted to teach music.

Then I asked myself, "What can I do that would be of the greatest benefit to the world?" I realized that there are already many great painters and fashion designers, but the ideas I had for teaching music were totally unique — and only I could give this gift to the world. That was the determining factor in my decision.

I was convinced that everyone should — and could — have the opportunity to receive a music education. And I felt that I was the one to provide them with that opportunity. So I went home to my parents and announced that I was going to write a course that would make it possible for everyone to teach themselves to read music and play the piano. And I began to write.

My parents were often dismayed and sometimes alarmed at my pursuits. But this was simply too much for them! They said it was impossible and unthinkable, and asked whatever gave me the idea that I could do something that nobody else had ever done. I found their opposition and resistance painful and stifling — and I felt trapped.

Previously, I had been taking flying lessons, which, when my parents found out about it, caused a situation that was intolerable. And the eruption brought about by my insisting on writing the Piano Course was comparable to the turmoil the flying lessons had created.

For several years, I had been writing a letter to God every morning, and I was following that practice at the time I announced that I was going to write the Piano Course. One morning, in my letter to God, I said, "Why can't Mother and Daddy understand that I just have to do this? If only they wouldn't resist what I am doing! I know I have to do it!"

While I was writing my letter to God on that particular morning, this came to me: "Their resistance is providing exactly what you need. After all, in order to rise, an airplane takes off into the wind." From then on, I no longer "resisted" their resistance. I felt at peace. And I continued to write the Piano Course. But I must add that I have long since realized, with regret, how difficult I made life for my parents.

Later, encouraged by eminent educators and professionals, and by the accomplishments of my students, I wrote, refined, and published *The McClintock Piano Course: A New Experience in Learning.* The Course enables anyone without previous knowledge of music or the keyboard to teach themselves to read music and play the piano.

Years ago, I studied improvisation with a great teacher, whose words confirmed my deepest inner feelings. He said, "Music is a game that God gave man to help him discover himself." That has been my real pursuit, "discovering myself" — and then finding ways to present the musical and spiritual principles I've experienced so that others can apply those same principles in their lives.

In my search to find the answers, I traveled various metaphysical and spiritual paths — never for the purpose of simply knowing about them, but to find and

apply the principles that the particular path presented.
When my search led me to the work of Joel S. Goldsmith
— a 20th century mystic — I felt I had come home.

Joel taught and lectured worldwide on the principles
of spiritual growth and development that were revealed
to him, and which he called "The Infinite Way."
Among his more than forty books are: *The Infinite
Way, The Art of Meditation, The Art of Spiritual
Healing, Practicing the Presence, The Contemplative
Life, The Thunder of Silence, The Mystical I, Living
Between Two Worlds,* and *The Altitude of Prayer.*

The pamphlet, *The Fourth Dimension of Life,* and
the book, *The Infinite Way,* were my introduction to
Joel's teachings. And I felt that this was the Path for me.
I attended Joel's classes and worked with him as a
student, both by correspondence and in person.

Each week, an Infinite Way Tape Meeting was held
here in New York. And from time to time, I conducted
some of the meetings — filling in for the individual
who was actually in charge of the activity. Conducting a
Tape Meeting involved beginning with a meditation,
then playing a tape of one of Joel's lectures or classes,
and concluding the meeting with another meditation.

Joel lived in Hawaii with his wife, Emma. It was
Emma's idea and firm conviction that the message must
be recorded and preserved. She traveled with Joel
around the world, recording his lectures and classes.
And she not only recorded the message, but also took

on the responsibility for the duplication and distribution of the tapes. Because of Emma's dedication, the message was made available for the students to study individually and at the Tape Meetings. Transcriptions of many of the recordings were, and are, published in Monthly Letters and in Joel's books. Thus, through the recordings and his books, the preservation of his work is assured.

In 1959, I attended a class that Joel gave in Hawaii. And while I was there, he asked me to arrange for the class and lectures that he was soon to give in New York. From then on, when he came to New York, I always took care of the arrangements, including the hotel reservations, the selection of the lecture halls, and the student registration for the classes.

The first time I made the arrangements, I had an announcement printed, which included the schedule and location of each of the lectures and of the class. And I prepared for Joel and Emma to arrive — placing flowers and fruit in the suite that I had chosen for them at the hotel. I met them at the airport and returned to the hotel with them.

Then I showed Joel the announcement I had had printed. He looked at it and said, "This is fine, but you will have to have it done over." I was shocked, and I asked, "Why?" He said, "You will have to add: For information concerning the Tape Meetings and the healing work, contact Lorene McClintock — and give your address and phone number."

I was stunned, and I said I really couldn't do that. So far, I had been willing to help out, but I had never thought of taking more responsibility than would be involved when Joel was here in New York. I was very busy writing my Piano Course, and I had just co-founded the New York City Opera Guild. Furthermore, I certainly didn't feel qualified to do healing work — and I told him so. Joel's reply was, "Anything you can't handle, just let me know."

Frankly, I was shaken up and scared, and I wondered how I had ever allowed this to happen to me. I realized that this was going to mean a total change in my life, and I didn't know how I could deal with it.

The first of the lectures was to be given at the Carnegie Recital Hall. And I discovered that I would have to go out on the stage to introduce Joel.

Before the lecture was to begin, Joel and I were sitting backstage meditating, and I was far more nervous than I had ever been before I was to give a piano concert.

Suddenly, the time arrived, and Joel said, "Are you ready?" And I quiveringly said, "Yes." Then Joel said, "Just remember, It always uses us exactly as we use a fountain pen." I was distracted for a moment by the profound analogy, and at the same time, I thought, "I just hope there is ink in it!" We walked out onto the stage — and my public association with Joel S. Goldsmith was established.

When Joel's work for that particular visit was completed, he told me that he was pleased with the job I had done. I went to the airport to see them off, and as they were leaving, he said he was counting on me. I wanted to cry. And then I remembered what he had said earlier: "If there is anything you can't handle, just let me know."

Following through with my commitment, I began to conduct a meeting each week at which I played a tape of one of Joel's lectures or classes, and at which, after a time, I began to offer suggestions for the application and practice of the principles of The Infinite Way. Out of this work with the students, evolved a series of fifteen lessons for Infinite Way study.

I began to teach some Infinite Way classes. And I continued to work on the Piano Course, which was an enormous project (201 lessons — with music and text). I was distressed, however, because Joel seemed impatient with me concerning my persistence in spending time with the Course. But I felt impelled to do it. Although he never spoke to me about abandoning the project, I knew that his wish to have me travel around the world and give Infinite Way classes placed my work on the Piano Course — in his estimation — below the bottom of the list.

During that time, I had an overwhelming conviction of the absolute necessity for love and forgiveness, and I was developing a unique methodology for practicing forgiveness. I was also having a startling revelation concerning Mind and the Garden of Eden. As each aspect of this work unfolded, I presented it to the students in the classes that I gave.

Then, in 1963, I went to Hawaii to attend a class of Joel's and to spend time with him and Emma. I took with me the lessons for Infinite Way study that I had written and the work I had — up to that time — completed on the Piano Course. I wanted Joel to see what I had done, and was doing. And I also was eager to tell him about the revelation I had had concerning the Garden of Eden, and about the unfoldment and development of my work on Mind, and Love and Forgiveness.

I began by showing Joel the lessons for Infinite Way study. I had not anticipated — let alone hoped — that he would be so enthusiastic. The students in New York had found the lessons to be extremely helpful, but I had no further plan concerning them. I was hardly prepared for Joel's response. He said, "These lessons must be made available for all the students." And then he said, "The work has come through your consciousness, so you should determine how the lessons should be presented."

We discussed and agreed that the lessons should be called "Assignments for Infinite Way Study." And we concluded that there should be a fee — which we decided upon. The lessons would not all be sent at one time. The first two lessons would be mailed separately and each would be studied for two weeks. The subsequent lessons would be mailed and studied weekly. Thus the entire course was to extend over a period of seventeen weeks. And it was to be made clear that the lessons were to be used only for individual study.

Then Joel said, "Have your lawyer prepare an agreement for me to sign, stating that you are to have the sole ownership of this Course, and that you are to secure the copyright in your name." I found all of this overwhelming. But when I returned to New York, I followed his suggestions. And I have a copy of the agreement that Joel signed. (Incidentally, since that time, the Assignments have been used by students around the world. Almost every week, I receive requests for the Course.)

After Joel had seen the Assignments, I showed him the part of the Piano Course that I had completed and had brought with me. When he read it, he said, "I had no idea! All the spiritual principles are in this Course. It will provide spiritual growth as well as enlightenment and fulfillment for anyone who works with it." Needless to say, I was overjoyed to at last have Joel understand why I had been so persistent in continuing the work on the Piano Course.

During the days that I sat with Joel in his office, I told him about the revelation I had had concerning the Garden of Eden, and about the development of the work on Love and Forgiveness, and how I was incorporating his statement about Mind. I also told him about my realization concerning a methodology for practicing forgiveness. I had been invited to give a class on the island of Maui, and I thought some of this work might come forth — which it did.

I felt assured about the work — and where the inspiration was coming from — but since most of it was new, I wanted to check it out with Joel. He listened with fascination — his eyes sparkling, as they often did when he was zeroing in on an idea — and then he took a deep breath and complimented me and my ability to teach. What an experience!

In 1964, Joel invited me to speak at a class he was to give in Chicago. For an announcement of the class, I was asked to submit a title for my talk. Since I couldn't predict what I would talk about, I chose as my subject, "Living in the Now."

At the class, Joel introduced and recommended the *Assignments for Infinite Way Study* to the students. And he designated me as one of the teachers qualified to teach his work. This was the last class that Joel gave in the United States.

I returned to New York, and in a few days, Joel and Emma stopped by here on their way to England. I went to the airport to see them off. And one of the last things Joel said to me was, "I don't know how you can do it all (The Infinite Way work and write the Piano Course too), but I know that you must do it." Two weeks later (June 17, 1964), in London, Joel made his transition.

Love and Forgiveness

A New Way to Live

Love Greets You

The year after Joel made his transition, I went to London to give a class. Joel had always wanted me to go to London, and he had said, "If I'm not here to take you, Emma will present you to the students."

Emma had been in England for a few weeks before I was scheduled to arrive in London, and I felt comfortable knowing that she and some of the students would meet me at the airport.

For about an hour, however, before we reached London, I had an indescribable experience with Joel's "presence." I had been feeling an emotion similar to stage fright at the thought of giving a class in London. But communing with Joel's "presence" gave me a calming reassurance, and I leaned back and meditated and rested. And just as we were coming in over London, I looked down at the city and the river, and I heard these words, "Love greets you."

I didn't know whether the words were being spoken to me, or whether they were welling up inside me as my greeting to London, or whether they were London's greeting to me.

For several months, "Love" had been the theme of all of my work with the students in New York. During that time, a definition for the word "love" came to me, and it was, "Love is an experience of oneness."

"Love greets you" stayed with me not only while I was in London, but also when I went on to Hamburg to give a class there.

When I returned to New York, I looked up the word "greet" in my *Etymological Dictionary* (book of word origins) because I felt that "Love (an experience of oneness) greets you" must have a significant message for me. I found that "greet" means "to straighten, or to lift up, that which has been bent." I certainly could understand what it means to experience the feeling of being "bent" or "bowed down" — as if by the gravity of the earth.

"Man of Earth"

When I thought of "the gravity of the earth," I recalled that Joel spoke of "man of earth." And he said that "man of earth is not under the law of God, and neither indeed can be." Then I thought, "'Man of earth' must mean a human being." I found that the root of the word "human" comes from the Latin word "humus," meaning "of the earth." Could it be possible that I am man of earth — not under the law of God — even though I am reading and studying and meditating every day?

Love — an experience of oneness — would lift me up from being "man of earth." But what does it really mean to "experience oneness"? At least I knew that "oneness" is the opposite of "separateness." And so if I am not experiencing oneness, I must be experiencing separateness. Then I looked up the original meaning of the word "oneness." And, under the heading of "oneness," I noticed the word "reunite," meaning "to bring together again," or "to make one again." I certainly had not expected to see the word "again." But how revealing! The word "again" obviously implies that there had, at one time, been an experience of oneness.

I asked myself: "Experiencing oneness" *with* what? "Experiencing separateness" *from* what? Although I felt that I was beginning to have an inkling of an idea, I still felt confused about what I could do to be able to know whether I was "experiencing separateness," or whether I was "experiencing oneness."

"Man Who Has His Being in Christ"

I discovered that Joel not only spoke of "man of earth" but also of "man who has his Being in Christ." We usually think of "Christ" as meaning the man, Jesus, and we often speak of Him as "Christ Jesus," or "Jesus, the Christ." But I knew that the word "Christ" also refers to "the Spirit of God in man." Of course, the Spirit of God was in Jesus. And He was consciously aware of His "oneness" with It. He had His Being in Christ.

Moses and Buddha, and all the great Lights and Mystics were also aware of the Spirit of God in them. And we have been told that the Spirit of God is in each of us, too — in you and in me. But I realized that unless and until I could become aware of It, and "experience oneness" with It, I would be "experiencing separateness" — and I would still just be "man of earth." I begged and asked as fervently as I knew how to have the secret revealed. How could I have what is known as "the Christ consciousness"? How could I have my Being in Christ?

The Answer Begins to Reveal Itself

Then I remembered that Jesus said, "It profiteth ye nothing to pray for your friends, pray for your enemies if *ye* would be the children of God." And of course, a child of God is "man who has his Being in Christ." I had several Bible passages that I often repeated like affirmations — as if I were trying to make them so. But this passage, "praying for my enemies," certainly had not been one of my favorites. I didn't have enemies to pray for anyway — I thought. However, the passage said, "Pray for your enemies, if ye would be the children of God." Not for them to be the children of God — but "If *ye* would be the children of God."

I wondered what the secret was. How could "praying for my enemies" enable me to be "a child of God" or "man who has his Being in Christ"? How could praying for my enemies enable me to "experience oneness" with them and with the Spirit of God Within My Own Being?

I felt that I had to be sure that I understood more clearly what it means "to experience oneness"— what it means "to love." Then something that I considered to be an explanation came to me: To love, to experience oneness, is to have a conscious feeling of connectedness. I began to see that praying for my enemies — whoever they are — might be the answer I had been looking for.

And then I thought of a vital passage that I had overlooked. How many times I had closed my eyes and meditated and meditated — forgetting that we are told, "If you come to the altar to pray, and remember that you have aught (anything) against any man, or if any man has aught against you, rise, make peace with your brother, and then return to the altar." Of course, if I have aught against anyone, or if anyone has aught against me, I am experiencing separateness. But, by making peace with them, I would be experiencing oneness. I would have "a conscious feeling of connectedness" with them.

I couldn't recall ever having thought of that passage before I began to meditate or pray. I certainly hadn't ever realized the significance of the passage. And neither had I realized the significance of the passage, "Pray for your enemies, if ye would be the children of God."

Just knowing the passages, however, could do nothing for me. I could see that it is not the passages that I know and can recite that can change my life, but it is what I do about the passages — what I realize and practice.

I had come this far, but what should I do now? I couldn't believe that I had any enemies. Actually, I had never even thought seriously about it. Any time the subject of enemies came up, I always thought, "I really don't have any enemies. Other people may have them, but I don't. I love everybody." But the passage said, "If ye would be the children of God, pray for your enemies." So this must mean that I have them.

Finding Out Who My Enemies Are

When I found that I obviously had enemies, I knew that I would have to discover who they were, and also how to pray for them. I kept wondering who my enemies were. Then it came to me that my enemies are "those from whom I feel separate." So, those I condemn or judge are my enemies! I could see that "praying for my enemies" and "making peace with them" were essential for establishing an experience of oneness not only with them, but also with the Spirit of God Within My Own Being.

The realization was so powerful, and I was so stunned, that it was more than I could comprehend at the time. I remember thinking, "I'm not sure that I want to go through with this. If I pray for my enemies, what if everything turns out better for them than for me?"

Even though I had been asking and begging for an answer, I would have felt far more comfortable not having made the discovery. The idea of not condemning or judging was so hard to accept that I made all kinds of excuses, and I actually attempted to ignore it. A part of me knew that if I really understood what all this meant, I would have to turn my life totally around. I wouldn't be who I was anymore!

Condemning, Judging, and Gossiping

I began to notice that I seemed to derive enjoyment from condemning and judging. Gossiping came under the same category. I almost felt called upon to do it, because everybody else did it. It made me feel as if I were "a member of the club." Down deep, however, I knew that I shouldn't do that anymore. But I did it anyway.

Condemning, judging, and gossiping were such a habit that they felt natural to me. I had become so accustomed to the feeling that often I wasn't even aware that I was doing it. And if I did "catch myself in the act," I felt totally justified, and could give very valid reasons.

Once, I was having a conversation with a woman who knew about my concern with condemnation and judgment. Suddenly she became conscious that she was condemning someone. And she said, "Well, I know I'm condemning her, but she needs it." I realized that I often felt the same way when I was condemning. I continued to condemn and judge and gossip — but I was becoming more aware that I was doing it.

It occurred to me that condemning, judging, and gossiping were a kind of "food" that had a tangy taste.

It was tantalizing and enticing, and in a peculiar way, I enjoyed it. But I was beginning to feel uncomfortable and somewhat guilty.

Although I knew that it was important not to condemn or judge, I hadn't allowed myself to face the fact that my condemning and judging were ensuring my "experience of separateness."

This wasn't something that I particularly wanted to think about, so I focused on something that was more appealing. I recalled that Jesus said, "The things that I do, ye shall do also, and even greater things shall ye do." And I took Him at His word. I thought, "Well, why not?" But then, I realized that if I accepted that part of what He said, I would have to accept the other things that He said as well. I asked myself, "Have I really been thinking that I could pick out the part that I like and ignore the rest?"

I thought, "I'll try to do what Jesus said to do — I'll try to pray for my enemies." But first, I'll have to find out exactly who my enemies are. Of course, I already felt that my enemies were those I condemn or judge. And when I began to think about it, it was obvious that I had more enemies than I had been aware of.

An idea came to me, and I decided to experiment with it. With my eyes closed, I allowed to well up within me the names of some of those I felt condemnation or judgment toward.

I went back over the day. . . .

I asked myself, "Is there someone who irritated or annoyed me?"

At first, this seemed uncomfortable and strange. But I knew that the only thing I was concerned about now was: "Who are my enemies? Who are those I have condemned or judged, or who are those I am condemning or judging?"

Then I went back over the week . . .

I asked myself, "Is there anyone who I feel is responsible for some misfortune? Is there someone that I am jealous of? Is there someone from whom I am expecting something — and who isn't following through? Is there anyone who has hurt my feelings? Is there anyone I blame for something? Is there someone that I just don't like?"

I continued for a while to let those I had condemned or judged, or whom I was condemning or judging, present themselves.

A Path to Follow

I remembered that Jesus said, "Love the Lord thy God with all thy heart, with all thy soul, and with all thy mind, and love thy neighbor as thyself." I saw clearly that to "love the Lord thy God" means to consciously feel "at one" with the Spirit of God Within My Own Being. And to "love my neighbor as myself" means that those I have condemned or judged are my "neighbor" and that I must feel totally "at one" with them — as if they were myself.

I remembered that Jesus also said, "Forgive seventy times seven." What a startling thought! Why hadn't "forgiveness" occurred to me before? And why was forgiveness so important that it would be necessary to forgive seventy times seven? I had already thought about condemning, judging, and gossiping, which produce an "experience of separateness." And I could now see that if I refused to forgive someone, I certainly would be "experiencing separateness." Then I knew that forgiveness was a key to the "experience of oneness." But what was I supposed to do in order to forgive? Surely, I couldn't just say, "I forgive you." Even though I hadn't thought about forgiveness before, I now realized that it was essential for me to find out "how to forgive."

I began to realize that Jesus was providing a Path for us to follow, and that He was outlining exactly what had to be done. I just had to discover a way to do it. I wanted to be shown a way — a clear and precise "Procedure for Forgiveness."

Preparation for the "Procedure for Forgiveness"

At this point, the preparation for the "Procedure for Forgiveness" began to unfold in my consciousness. I found that I had to begin by writing down the names of all of those I could recall that I had ever condemned or

judged — or that I was condemning or judging —
consciously admitting that I had been (or was)
condemning or judging them.

So, I began to write down the names. Earlier, when
I had thought of only one name at a time, it wasn't so bad.
But when I saw the names written down — one name,
and another name, and another name, and on, and on, and
on — I couldn't believe what I was discovering. It was
such a shock that it was almost more than I could stand.

And, as if this were not enough, I then had one of
the most shattering experiences of my life! I realized
that I had been studying metaphysical, spiritual, and
mystical teachings for years, and I was even teaching
spiritual principles, myself. But it had never occurred to
me that I not only had been ignoring, but actually
violating, the very first — and most important —
principle for experiencing oneness with the Spirit of God
Within My Own Being. I felt such an overwhelming
sense of shame and remorse that I cried for two weeks.
The humiliation and embarrassment were indescribable.
And then it came to me: "Don't wallow in this! Don't
dramatize it! Let the experience turn to joy, because at
least the light is coming."

More Light Did Come

I was perplexed and confused, however, because in the
midst of this devastating experience, I found that I was
becoming aware of so much that nobody that I knew of

had apparently ever written or talked about. I saw how the sense of separation from my neighbor and from God (The Infinite Invisible Source Within My Own Being) had taken place, and how it had set up the experience in which I was living as "man of earth."

I also recognized that non-condemnation, non-judgment, and forgiveness would enable me to establish a conscious feeling of "connectedness" with my neighbor and with the Source Within My Own Being — which would allow me to live as "man who has his Being in Christ."

I knew that forgiveness contained a liberating secret, and that I was being given a detailed step-by-step Procedure, which — if followed — would bring freedom not only to me but to all mankind as well. This took place more than thirty years ago, before forgiveness had become the "household word" that it is today. It may be hard to believe, but any time I even hinted at the word "forgiveness," I met with such violent opposition and resistance that I quickly retreated.

So what was I to do? I kept it sacred and secret in my heart and in my consciousness — living with it and practicing it and experiencing it — until, reluctantly, I accepted the assurance that I was to release this message to the world.

Taking a Bold Step

I don't recall what year it was, but it was the Easter season, and I was deeply touched by the significance of the symbolism. At The Infinite Way Tape Meeting on the Thursday evening before Easter Sunday, I prepared to play Joel's tape concerning Maundy Thursday.

I always associated Maundy Thursday with the fact that Jesus washed the feet of His disciples on that day. The accepted interpretation of Jesus' washing the feet was an illustration of His humility. But my interpretation of the symbolism was different. I remember thinking that the feet are the part of us that touch the earth. As you know, earlier I discovered that the root of the word "human" comes from the Latin word "humus," meaning "of the earth." So, to me, Jesus' washing the feet of his disciples symbolized that He was "washing away their humanhood," or cleansing and purifying their consciousness. I was deeply affected by the realization that my own consciousness must be cleansed and purified.

By now, I was consumed with the awareness of the effect of condemning and judging, and with the development of the Procedure for Forgiveness. And I felt that this would be an appropriate — or at least an acceptable — time to present the preparation for the Procedure for Forgiveness to the students.

Before I played Joel's tape, I gave a short talk using my interpretation of the significance of Maundy Thursday. Although I was hesitant, apprehensive, and almost fearful of the reaction of the students, I took a bold step: As an assignment for the following week, I asked the students to write down the names of as many as they could remember that they had ever condemned or judged, or were condemning or judging.

Later, several of the students said to me, "This may be all right for some people, but it just isn't for me." Other students said, "I'm beyond all this! But how I wish my friends could hear it! It would help them so much!" I could identify with that remark, because I recalled that many times when I attended lectures and meetings, I would sit there the whole time "piping off" to someone else what I was hearing — thinking how great this message would be for them — and missing the whole point for myself.

Some students wrote me letters, "telling me off" — and asking me who I thought I was. But one young man said to himself, "Well, I've always done everything she has told me to do, so I will do it. I will start writing the names." And he said he had 160 names before he went to bed that night.

When We Condemn or Judge

Are you asking yourself, "Why should I do this — thinking of the names of all those I've condemned or judged? Why would I want to go back into the past, when we are told to live in the Now?" At first, I asked that question, too. But then I saw that the moment I condemned or judged or refused to forgive someone, I was feeling separate from them, and I was putting them into "prison" and locking them up. And no matter how long ago it was, they are still there — and will remain there — until I consciously release them. But if there is anyone, anywhere, whom I am refusing to release from the prison of my condemnation and judgment, I am separating myself not only from them, but also from the Spirit of God Within My Own Being.

Many times, I have closed my eyes and said, "Just let the Spirit flow — let the Spirit of God flow freely out to the world, and to anyone who presents themselves to my consciousness." Often, when I've done this, I've observed that I will think of someone, and I will just want to put them off to the side so they won't get the full flow — the full benefit. When I've caught myself doing this, I've had to ask, "Am I being an instrument through which the Spirit is flowing forth to the world? Is this 'man who has his Being in Christ'— isolating someone and saying: 'Not you, you can't have the fullness.'?"

I want to speak again about "going back into the past." When we began this work, some students said, "I don't even want to think about them, let alone dig up the past. I can't do that, because I have just now come to the point where I can see them in their Christhood." "Seeing someone in his or her Christhood" does not mean that we physically see them in a special way, but it means that we are acknowledging their True Identity — we are recognizing that the Spirit of God (The Infinite Invisible Source) dwells Within Their Being.

I don't believe that we can see anyone in his or her Christhood (their True Identity), or acknowledge that the Spirit of God dwells Within them, if we don't even want to think about them. If we love someone, do we hesitate to think about them? If we love them, we don't hesitate to bring them up out of the past, do we? It's only those that we are still condemning and judging, or refusing to forgive that we don't want to think about.

The list of ways we condemn or judge is staggering! We condemn or judge others for doing something that we think they should not do, or for not doing something that we think they should do. We condemn them for being thoughtless, inconsiderate, insensitive, or selfish. We may condemn them for saying or doing something that we feel we simply "can never forgive."

It isn't easy to face what has been going on within us. And we may prefer just to read about it. But unless we do what we know to do, we will not have the liberating experience that is available.

Further Preparation for the Procedure for Forgiveness

So now, it's time for you to begin to write down the names of some of those you have condemned or judged, or are condemning or judging, or refusing to forgive. Don't be surprised if there is a shock followed by a terrific feeling of remorse. I've told you that it hit me hard. But we have to feel such an urge to clear up everything so completely that we are willing to go all the way.

When I began to write down the names of all those I had condemned or judged, I thought, "If I had known anyone who had condemned or judged as many people as I had, I wouldn't have wanted to associate with them." I discovered that I had condemned or judged almost everybody I had ever known. And then I said, "Oh, well, now I see that I have condemned or judged everybody, so there's no point in going through with this." Others have told me that they've had the same experience. But that doesn't get us off the hook.

A Chance to Redeem a Lifetime

We now have an opportunity to redeem a lifetime. This is a chance to clear it all up. We may have failed before, but this gives us another chance.

You may say, "But this really is hopeless! I've condemned or judged everybody. How can I be forgiven for doing this? I'm the guilty one. How can I forgive myself?" I certainly do know the feeling!

Realizing That I Can't Forgive Myself

Then I realized something even more shocking: "I can't forgive myself!" There is no way that I can forgive myself. But do you recall that Jesus said, "Forgive us our debts as we forgive our debtors."? In other words, I can't forgive myself, but as I forgive others, I am forgiven.

I began to see that when someone hurt me or did harm to me, they were actually giving me a great opportunity. Because, since I have so much to be forgiven for and if I can be forgiven only as I forgive, this could provide me with a chance to "cancel out" a lot for myself.

Still Further Preparation for the Procedure for Forgiveness: I Begin to Get an Idea of How I Can Forgive

When I wrote the names of those I had condemned or judged, I realized that I had found out who my enemies were — at least some of them — but I had to find out more about how to forgive them. I knew that Jesus had very clearly and unmistakably said, "Forgive seventy times seven," and that He also had said, "Forgive us our debts as (in the degree that) we forgive our debtors." So I had no choice! But I would have to find out *how* to forgive. I would have to find "a way."

Then, still further preparation for the Procedure for Forgiveness began to reveal itself to me. I found that a way I was able to begin to forgive was this: I thought of something I had done that I wished I hadn't done — not necessarily the same thing that the person that I was condemning had done, but just something I wished I hadn't done — and that I wanted to be forgiven for. And then I said to myself, "What made me do that? I have no idea what made me do it. Something just got into me. I see now that I wouldn't have done it — if I could have kept from it. It's as if something just 'took over.' Whatever I did seems totally foreign to me now."

When I thought of experiences that I'd had, I could understand that what the person that I was condemning or judging had done was just as foreign to him or her as what I had done was foreign to me. Something must have just "taken over" in them, too. And, on this level, I actually had a "feeling of oneness"— of sorts — with the person I had been condemning. I could see that we both had been "in the same boat."

Have you ever done something or said something, and immediately regretted it? And did you feel so bad and embarrassed about it that you would have given anything just to be able to back up and cancel it out and pretend that it had never happened? If you've ever had such an experience, you may have said, or at least felt, "Why on earth did I do that? I don't know why I did it." Once, when this happened to me, I wondered whether this could be what Jesus meant when he said, "They know not what they do."

When I am judging or condemning someone, I've often said, "That's not like them!" But I never understood what that meant until I had the experience of seeing that something that I had done just didn't seem like me either. But I had done it! And I wanted to be forgiven for it. Then I remembered the passage, which is a quotation from the Apostle Paul: "I don't sin, but there is a sense of sin in me." That passage itself shows that it is not really a part of us, but it is something that is functioning through us.

What We Do to Ourselves When We Condemn, Judge, or Refuse to Forgive

If we condemn, judge, gossip, or refuse to forgive, we often feel uncomfortable, or guilty, or sad, or disgruntled, or angry. We feel all these emotions because there is an area of our consciousness where we know that if we are allowing condemnation, judgment, gossip, or lack of forgiveness to function in us, we are separating ourselves from the Source.

Have you ever known anyone who constantly complains? Complaining is the fuel that runs their "motor." Complaining is a disguise for condemnation and judgment, and it intensifies and perpetuates an "experience of separateness."

If we are complaining, we are functioning on a level where we are completely open to all kinds of difficulties — which simply pour through us as our experiences. We are operating on the level where all the problems and miseries of humanhood exist. And we are susceptible to anything and everything that happens to come along.

When you are having difficulties and problems, have you ever thought, "Why is this happening to me?" Or have you felt that somehow you are "unlucky" or "getting a raw deal" or that "it's just not fair"? If you observe yourself saying or thinking something like that, look deeply as you ask yourself, "Am I blaming someone or something for the situation in which I'm finding myself?" You may be surprised to discover that you are condemning, judging, or refusing to forgive.

Or, if you are faced with a situation that you just can't handle, have you ever wondered whether God is giving you a challenge to meet, or whether He is punishing you for your "bad deeds"? We really can't ever blame God. Because, in the first place, God doesn't punish! But neither does God reward! There isn't a God sitting off someplace, like a "giant puppeteer," manipulating the strings, and doling out rewards and punishments. Always remember that God is "The Infinite Invisible."

The Choice Is Ours

It is shocking to discover that the choice is ours, and it has been ours all the time. We choose the frequency on which we operate. There are two frequencies or channels, and each has its own characteristics and conditions. We, ourselves, switch a particular channel on or off. We can function on one channel or frequency as "man of earth, not under the law of God" — experiencing separateness as we are cut off from our neighbor and from the Source.

Or, we can function on the other channel or frequency as "the child of God, or man who has his Being in Christ" — experiencing oneness with our neighbor and with the Source — as we let the Spirit flow through us, and as us.

It's pretty obvious which channel we are tuned in to most of the time. But the requirement for changing channels is very clear. The secret that will keep us attuned to our neighbor and to the Source is non-condemnation, non-judgment, and forgiveness.

Beginning to Use Some of the Steps of the Procedure for Forgiveness

Earlier, we wrote down the names of some of those we've condemned or judged, or are condemning or judging. But now we will write the names in a different way, because we are going to begin to use some of the steps of the Procedure for Forgiveness.

You will need some sheets of paper or a notebook and a pen or pencil. We not only are going to write the names of those we have condemned or judged, or are condemning or judging, but we are going to make other lists as well. So you will need lots of paper. You will continue to add to your lists for a long time. As a matter of fact, I haven't known anyone yet who has "graduated" — and that includes me! We just keep finding more names to add almost daily.

To begin, you will write a list of the names of those

you've condemned or judged, or are condemning or judging "for doing something." And then you will write a list of the names of those you've condemned or judged, or are condemning or judging "for not doing something."

Now write a heading for each of the two categories — using a separate page for each heading. (Leave plenty of room below each heading to write lots of names):

(1) **"For something they did, or are doing,"** and

(2) **"For something they didn't do, or aren't doing."**

And now, begin to write the names, placing each name under the proper heading. You don't need to write what you have been — or are — condemning or judging them for. That is, it isn't necessary to write down what they did or didn't do — just their name is sufficient. But you may find that you may need to place the same name under each of the two headings — something they did, and something they didn't do. Just keep pouring the names out. When you have written as many names as you can recall, stop for a while — realizing that you will add many more names from time to time.

Did you think of those whose names you hesitate to put on the list?

Maybe you should have started your list with·my name. And maybe you did! Did you think of members of your family, and those you see every day as well as those you remember from the past — perhaps those who are no longer on this plane? There may be those whose names you've forgotten, or those whose names you never knew. But there will be some way that you can identify them on the lists. Someone may have turned in front of you on the highway or on the street without putting on the signal light, or someone may have rushed in ahead of you when you had been waiting in line. You may remember some salesperson whose unpleasant behavior irritated you; or you may remember a workman who didn't come when he said he would, or who didn't do a good job when he finally did show up. And of course, there are many opportunities for names to put on your lists as you read or watch "the news."

At this point, don't be concerned about the details of how to forgive them. It is important, however, to remember that it is our *own* consciousness that we are dealing with. This is where we are clearing it all out. It is for ourselves that we forgive others.

And now you will write a list of "the things you have done that you wish you hadn't done," and another list of "the things you didn't do that you wish you had done."

On separate pages, write a heading for each of the two categories — leaving plenty of room to write below each heading:

(1) **"Things I've done that I wish I hadn't done,"** and

(2) **"Things I didn't do that I wish I had done."**

Before you read on, write — below the proper heading — as many things as you can recall that you've done that you wish you hadn't done, and as many things as you can recall that you didn't do that you wish you had done.

Did you find that you couldn't think of many things that you've done or haven't done to put on your lists? It's amazing, isn't it! We may get more things to put on our list by thinking of things that others could put on a list for us. So we can turn it back in the other direction and see what somebody else might wish to have us put down.

When you have written a lot of things under each heading — the things you've done that you wish you hadn't done, and the things you didn't do that you wish you had done — you are ready to begin the work with the lists.

How to Work With the Lists

Now, look at the first name on the list of those that you've condemned or judged, or are condemning or judging, *for doing something*. As you look at the name, think of the individual and what they did, or are doing — just for an instant — but don't dwell on it. Immediately turn your attention away from them, and look at the list of *things you've done* that you wish you hadn't done, and choose one specific thing.

What you choose does not need to relate to the person that you are condemning or judging, and neither does it need to be the same kind of thing that they did. It is easy to forget this, and to spend a lot of time trying to find something that is exactly the same as the other person did.

Often, students have said, "But I've never done anything as bad as that person did." This has nothing to do with whether we did anything that bad or not. We have done things that probably are just as bad from our level of consciousness. Some have said, "But I've never murdered anybody." Well, is it possible that we may have murdered them in our hearts or in our thoughts? It is whatever we have felt or done in our hearts or in our thoughts that we are responsible for.

Just remember, however, to choose something — anything — that you've done that you wish you hadn't done. But, for now, don't choose something that you *didn't do* that you wish you had done.

Then ask yourself, "What made me do it? Why did I do that?" And then do you know what you may say? "I don't know why I did it. Something just took over." And often you may say, "At the time, I felt totally justified in doing what I did. I wish now that I hadn't done it. But that's the way it was, and I want to be forgiven for it."

By now, I can see that what the other person did was not "of them" any more than what I did was "of me." It seems that neither of us could help doing what we did at the time. When I come to this point, I often want to reach out for their hand to acknowledge a feeling of "oneness," because I know that we have both been victimized by something that really isn't "of us." However, even though what I did was not "of me," I allowed it to function through me, and therefore, I am responsible, and I must be forgiven for it.

I know that I can't forgive myself — but what can I do? Why is it so hard to remember what Jesus said? Of course, He said, "Forgive us our debts as we forgive our debtors." Wasn't He saying that unless I forgive, I, myself, won't be forgiven?

Sometimes I want to cry — and sometimes, I do. It's quite a shattering experience to discover what has been going on within us without our even being aware of it! I said earlier that I feel it is all right to experience regret and remorse when we see what we have done. But we shouldn't exaggerate our "suffering." We should use the experience as an example that enables us to forgive someone else.

There are other steps of the Procedure for Forgiveness that we will discuss later. For the present, however, continue to work in the same way with the names on your list of those you have condemned, or are condemning, for doing something, as you choose something from your own list of things you've done that you wish you hadn't done.

And then, work with the names on the list of those you have condemned, or are condemning, for not doing something, as you choose something from your own list of things you didn't do that you wish you had done.

Ultimately, you should use the suggested Procedure as you work with each name on your lists. However, when you have worked with a "substantial" number of names, you may wish to rest for a while before you continue.

When I Separate Myself From the Source

Do I realize that each time I condemn, judge, or refuse to forgive someone, I not only am separating myself from them, but I am also separating myself from The Infinite Invisible Source — the Spirit of God Within My Own Being?

This is all so difficult to accept that we usually don't even "hear" the words we are reading. When I say, "I separate myself from the Source, or that I separate myself from the Spirit of God Within My Own Being," do I realize what this means? It means that I am cut off from the Source — the Infinite, Invisible Spiritual Energy — which is the Life Force of My Being. When I separate myself from the Source, I turn off the switch, and "the lights are out." I am fumbling around in the dark — open to anything in the human scene that happens to be out there. It doesn't discriminate!

"Awake thou that sleepest, and Christ will give thee light." Using the steps of the Procedure for working with the lists is a way to help us awaken. As we work with the lists, however, we must always be alert to catch ourselves in the act of saying, "How can I ever forgive myself?" We now know that we can't forgive ourselves, but that we can be forgiven only as (in the degree that) we forgive others.

Earlier, we asked if you had ever done something, and afterward, could not believe that you had done it. And you felt absolutely miserable, and wondered what

on earth you could do about it. You knew that you
couldn't forgive yourself, and so you simply prolonged
the agony. But did you realize what you could do? Here
is the answer to always remember: "Think of someone
that you feel you can't possibly forgive, and forgive them!"

Catching Ourselves in the Act

Even though we are beginning to recognize — and
admit — how much we have judged, and condemned,
and refused to forgive, and even though we are in the
midst of clearing it all out, we are often shocked at the
persistence of the habit.

There are stories that I tell about experiences of
some of the students in New York. One student went
into St. Thomas Church on Fifth Avenue and sat down
to meditate and "work on his list." ("Working on the
list" has come to mean going through the list of names,
and using the familiar steps of the Procedure for
Forgiveness — adding other names as they present
themselves.) The student was alone in this vast church.
Then, "out of nowhere," the janitor appeared. And the
only place that he found in the entire church that was
dirty and needed cleaning was on the floor right beside
the feet of the student. As the janitor was scraping away,
the student became more and more disturbed, and
more and more annoyed. And he said to himself, "I'm
sitting here forgiving, and this man has the nerve to
pick out this one place in the whole church where he

decides to do his scrubbing." And he said that he got up to "storm out" before he realized what he was doing.

This is how quickly our old habit takes over. We think we are forgiving one person, and somebody else comes up, and we condemn or judge them, without even realizing it.

In New York, at one of our Thursday Evening Tape Meetings, which were held at a hotel, I had been presenting this work to the students. And we were sitting in silence just letting love (an experience of oneness) and forgiveness flow out to all those in the room and on out to the world. Earlier, we had ordered some coat hangers, since we didn't have any in the room. And about this time, the door opened with a squeak, and the man came "clanking" in with the coat hangers. You could just feel the whole room become tense as everybody was thinking, with indignation, "The very idea of anybody entering at this point, when we are sitting here forgiving!"

I tell these stories because they help us "catch ourselves." We may know that we do something, or we may recall an incident or two, but that won't do any good. We may "know" that we do it, but it is "catching ourselves in the act" of judging or condemning — right there in the split second — that is the only way to stop it. Because it's a habit. Something just "takes over" and we automatically get "carried away."

I feel so strongly about this that I want to mention it again. Simply "knowing that we do something" that we want not to do is not sufficient. I found this in teaching piano. I would say to students, "This is the correct way to do it, and this way is incorrect." And they seemed to understand. But until they "caught themselves in the act" of doing it incorrectly, they couldn't break the habit. In the split second that we catch ourselves, however, something that seems like an electrical current goes through us — and the habit is erased.

We know that Jesus said, "Forgive seventy times seven," which indicates that He knew that we would be having problems. He was actually telling us that we shouldn't be discouraged if we couldn't totally forgive the first time we tried, but that it might take seventy times seven. Do you realize how many times that is? It's four hundred and ninety times! We have to forgive again and again and again until we have established an "experience of oneness" — which is love.

Another admonition that Jesus gave us relates directly to condemning and judging. And we usually remember only the first part of the passage: "Agree with thine adversary quickly." If we think of, or repeat, the passage, we are apt to leave off the "quickly," which really is the key. When we are tempted to condemn or judge, we must catch ourselves *instantly* and refuse to react or resist, but instead, to quickly yield, or "let it be." Otherwise, we not only will have more to forgive, but also more to be forgiven for.

Looking for a Solution to the "Puzzle of Separateness"

Of course, if I am condemning, or judging, or refusing to forgive, I am experiencing "separateness" — and the theme of this work is "oneness." Obviously, forgiveness, non-condemnation, and non-judgment are the answer. But I wanted to understand more. I wanted to know how we got into this "predicament of humanhood."

For me to understand how and why forgiveness, non-condemnation, and non-judgment are such an essential part of establishing an "experience of oneness," I felt that I had to know how the "experience of separateness" had come about. And to uncover the part of the puzzle that would help me find the solution, I needed to back up, and begin at the beginning, where the departure from the "experience of oneness" first took place. So I began with the Garden of Eden.

My interpretation of the Garden of Eden is in the form of an allegory. That is, it is a story or description in which the characters and events symbolize a deeper underlying meaning.

The Garden of Eden

The Garden of Eden Is a Place of Spiritual Delight

Now, I'm going to talk about the Garden of Eden. In the second chapter of Genesis, we are told that the Lord God planted a Garden "eastward in Eden." The esoteric meaning of "eastward" is "spiritual," and the original or esoteric meaning of "Eden" is "delight." The Garden of Eden is a place of "spiritual delight." It is a state of consciousness — a state of pure bliss — unconditioned consciousness. And the Lord God placed man in the Garden of Eden — in this state of bliss.

The Lord God's Admonition

"The Lord God commanded the man, saying: Of every tree of the Garden, thou mayest freely eat. But of the tree of the knowledge of good and evil, thou shalt not eat of it. For in the day that thou eatest thereof, thou shalt surely die."

An Explanation of Mind

Before we proceed, I must tell you that there is a statement that Joel gave us about "mind" that provides a part of the foundation for my interpretation of the Garden of Eden. This statement appears in Joel Goldsmith's book, *The Thunder of Silence*. Here is the statement: "Mind is an avenue or an instrument of awareness." You will understand the statement more fully as we go along.

In my interpretation of the Garden of Eden, I refer to "mind" as symbolizing man. So "mind" (or man) was placed in the Garden, in a state of bliss. Here again, is the statement about mind that was mentioned earlier: "Mind is an avenue or an instrument of awareness." If we think of "mind" as an instrument or an avenue of awareness, we can imagine it as a conduit (or a pipe) that is placed or "set down" in this state of spiritual bliss — unconditioned consciousness. And this unconditioned consciousness is pouring forth from the Source through the mind (the conduit), forming itself as unconditioned form. When we use the word "unconditioned," we mean "pure, unlimited, and unaffected or conditioned by what we term good and evil."

Unconditioned Consciousness

If the words "unconditioned consciousness" do not seem clear to you, think of "pure Invisible Spiritual Energy." Everything is energy, and everything — every form — has its own vibration. When we say that this Energy (this Invisible Spiritual Substance) is pouring through the mind — forming Itself as unconditioned form — we can think of the Energy, or the vibrational frequency, as being "lowered" or "slowed down" or "stepped down" to the point at which It can be seen as form.

An illustration that I always think of relates to my taking flying lessons years ago. The plane that I flew had propellers. When the propellers rotated at maximum speed, I couldn't see that they were there at all. They were literally invisible. Then, when I shut off the engine, the rate of speed gradually decreased until I could clearly see each rotation of the propellers.

You've probably noticed this phenomenon when you've turned on a fan at high speed, and have become aware that you couldn't see the blades at all. But then, when you shut the fan off, the blades rotated slower and slower until each individual blade became distinctly visible.

You can understand how the same principle applies to the unconditioned consciousness (The Invisible Spiritual Energy). When the rate of the vibration of the Energy is "lowered," or "slowed down" sufficiently, it becomes visible form. This explanation should help clarify the earlier paragraphs with the statements concerning mind and unconditioned consciousness. I suggest that you reread the three preceding paragraphs, and then read this paragraph again.

The Mind's Attention Is Centered on the Spirit Within

The mind should always turn its attention inward — looking only to the Spirit, or the Source. The attention remains centered within, in a state of bliss, as the unconditioned consciousness flows forth from the

Source — through the mind — forming itself as unconditioned form.

A Helpmate Is Needed

Now, we are told that a helpmate was needed for man (or mind). You see, all this time, the unconditioned consciousness has been flowing forth from the Source through the mind (the conduit), and forming itself as unconditioned form. But there has been no means by which the form could be experienced. And that is why a helpmate was needed.

And so a rib was taken from man (mind) to form the helpmate. The esoteric, or original, meaning of the word "rib" is "a portion or a compartment." A portion or a compartment of the mind (man) was taken to form the helpmate (woman). The helpmate was the intellect and the senses, which could now experience that which was being formed. The mind's attention is turned within toward the Spirit, and the intellect and the senses have been provided to experience "the outer — that which is being formed."

A Review

Let's review what has happened so far: There is the unconditioned state of consciousness, with the mind planted in it. The mind's attention is always to be turned inward toward the Spirit, or the Source. The unconditioned consciousness flows forth through the mind (the conduit), forming itself as unconditioned form. And, to experience that which is being formed, the helpmate or woman (the intellect and the senses) has been provided.

The Man and the Woman Were Naked and Not Ashamed

The man (mind) and the helpmate or woman (the intellect and the senses) were always to be together — "at one" with the Source. They were in the Garden, in a state of bliss. And "they were naked, and not ashamed."

My interpretation of "they were naked and not ashamed" is that since they were "at one" with the Source, there was no necessity to "add" to themselves, either for enhancement or protection. There was nothing to be desired or feared because they were totally fulfilled and secure. Therefore, they did not need to cover or clothe themselves with concepts, opinions, or judgments. They were "experiencing oneness" with the Source, and they were pure and complete — naked and not ashamed. They were simply abiding in a state of "Is."

A Reminder of the Lord God's Admonition

As you know, the Lord God had told them that they could eat of all the trees in the Garden except the tree of the knowledge of good and evil. But if they ate of

that tree, they would surely die. My interpretation of
the Lord God's admonition is that if they judged good
or evil, they would die or be cut off from the Source. In
other words, they would no longer "experience oneness"
with the Source or with the Spirit of God Within Their
Own Being, but they would "experience separateness."

An Explanation of "the Serpent "

At the beginning of the third chapter of Genesis, we are
told that the serpent was the most subtle of all the
beasts. I found that the esoteric meaning of "serpent" is
"separateness or apartness." And the definition of
"subtle" is "difficult to detect and crafty." Since the
serpent is difficult to detect and crafty, he presents
himself as an appearance or an illusion of separateness.

The Serpent Contradicts the
Lord God's Admonition

The serpent (the sense of separation) asked her (the
intellect and the senses) if she couldn't eat of all the trees
in the Garden. And she said, "We can eat of all the trees
except one. We can't eat of the fruit of the tree of the
knowledge of good and evil — we can't even touch it
— or we will surely die." The serpent was crafty, and he
contradicted the Lord God's admonition. He said, "If
you eat of the tree of the knowledge of good and evil,
you not only won't die, your eyes will be opened, and

you will be as gods, knowing good and evil." Knowing good and evil meant that they would have the ability to judge that which is good and that which is evil. Thus they could determine what was an advantage or what was a threat to them. It is important to remember that it is the serpent (the sense of separation) that is "planting" this idea.

The Effect of the Serpent's Contradiction of the Lord God's Admonition

You see, the unconditioned consciousness is flowing through the mind and forming itself as unconditioned form, which the intellect and the senses are now experiencing. They are in a state of bliss — "experiencing oneness" with the Source, and with All That Is. But when the serpent (the sense of separation) contradicted the Lord God's admonition, he fooled them, and they forgot that they were still "at one" with the Source, and with All That Is. And so when they looked at that which was being formed, it suddenly *appeared* to be separate from them.

We Aren't Separate, We Only Appear to Be Separate

As we look at each other, we "seem" to be separate. We forget that we are one. It just looks as if we were separate. We all come from the same Source — the same Invisible Spiritual Energy — but we each have our own individual vibration. It's because we are in "packages" or bodies that makes it look as if we were separate. We aren't separate, any more than the branches of a tree are separate from the tree. And because the branches are one with the tree, they are one with each other.

There is no separateness — never has been — never can be. Of course, we are one with each other. But it is the subtlety — the illusion — that makes us believe that we are separate.

Whatever Appears to Be Separate From Me May Be an Advantage or a Threat

When I see something that I believe is separate from me, I will think of it as having the possibility of being an advantage or a threat. That is, when I no longer have the feeling of "oneness" or "connectedness" with it, automatically it will have the quality of good or of evil. As long as I feel "at one" with it, however, it does not have those qualities.

When They Were "at One" With the Source They Were Naked — Pure and Complete

Earlier, we found that when they were naked, they were pure and complete — experiencing oneness with the Source. They were "at one" with the Source, and "at one" with all that was flowing forth as unconditioned form. They had no sense of separation from anything. And of course, there was no necessity to appropriate or add to themselves, or to protect or defend themselves.

She (the Intellect and the Senses) Sees the Fruit of the Tree as Something That She Can Appropriate

As you recall, she (the intellect and the senses) said to the serpent (the sense of separation), "If we eat of the fruit of the tree of the knowledge of good and evil, we will surely die." (That is, they would be cut off or separate from the Source.) And the serpent (the sense of separation) replied, "You not only won't die, your eyes will be opened, and you will be as gods — knowing (or being able to judge) good and evil." And of course, we judge as good or evil only that which "appears" to be separate from us. Then she looked at the fruit of the tree, and she saw it as something separate from her that she could appropriate, or add to herself. And so she judged it as "good" — an advantage.

Forgetting the Lord God's Admonition, She "Falls for" the Serpent's Temptation

"When she (the intellect and the senses) saw that the tree was good for food, and that it was *pleasant* to the eyes, and a tree to be *desired* to make one wise, she took of the fruit thereof, and did eat, and gave it to her husband with her."

Now That They Have Eaten of the Fruit, They Must Cover or Clothe Themselves

When they ate of the fruit of the tree of the knowledge of good and evil, they cut themselves off from the Source, and they experienced separateness. So, in order to determine that which is an advantage or a threat, they must now clothe or cover themselves with concepts, opinions, and judgments.

Sewing Fig Leaves Together to Make Themselves Aprons

We are told that they sewed fig leaves together to make themselves aprons. When I first became involved with this exploration and search concerning the Garden of Eden, I wondered what was meant by "They sewed fig leaves together and made themselves aprons." I found that the original, or esoteric, meaning of the word "apron" is a "map."

I envisioned a map, like a circuit map used by telephone companies, with electrical currents forming patterns — corresponding to the veins in the fig leaves. A thought produced by the intellect follows a particular path — like the pattern made by the electrical current on the circuit map. Each repetition of a thought initiates the same impulse — "setting off" the current, which follows and deepens the identical pattern.

Of course, now that they have "sewed fig leaves together and made themselves aprons," they will no longer remain naked. But they will cover or clothe themselves with concepts, beliefs, opinions, judgments, and convictions, thus enabling them to automatically judge good and evil.

Beliefs, Concepts, Opinions, Judgments, and Convictions

Continuous repetition of a thought establishes a belief. And continuous repetition of a belief establishes a concept, an opinion, or a judgment. A thought "triggered" by an emotion or feeling not only follows a particular pattern made by the electrical current on the circuit map, but the emotion or feeling intensifies the pattern.

We can see how — without realizing it — we establish sets of beliefs, opinions, judgments, and convictions that we unconsciously act upon, thereby permitting them to govern our lives.

Patterns of Thoughts and Emotions

When strong emotions or feelings (such as anger, hate, envy, jealousy, desire or fear) accompany the thoughts,

deep and vivid patterns are established on the circuit
map. These patterns form firm beliefs, concepts, opinions,
judgments, and convictions, which can be erased only
by non-judgment, non-condemnation, and forgiveness
— and by consciously reestablishing an "experience of
oneness."

   These patterns of thoughts and emotions, which
establish sets of beliefs and convictions, are not always
"negative." They can be "positive" as well. But they are
never of the Spirit, because they are based on that
which is "outside," or that from which we feel separate
or apart. Even if we have "beliefs and convictions"
about God, we are feeling separate and apart from God.
And when we feel separate or apart from God, that God
will have the qualities of good and evil (an advantage or
a threat). In other words, that God will have the
possibility of doing us a favor or of punishing us. Our
"experience of oneness" with God or The Infinite Invisible
Source, however, is not a set of beliefs or convictions,
but a *realization* — or a *conscious knowingness.*

Man Hides From the Lord God

After they had sewed fig leaves together and made
themselves aprons, they heard the voice of the Lord
God walking in the Garden. And the Lord God called
to the man (the mind) and said, "Where are you?" And
he (the man) said, "I heard Your voice, and I was afraid
because I was naked, and I hid myself."

He realized that he had been naked — pure and complete. But when he said, "I heard Your voice," he was indicating that he was aware that he was now separate from the Lord God. And since he felt separate, he hid himself. That is, he clothed or covered himself with concepts, and he judged the encounter as bad (a threat). Therefore he was afraid, because he feared punishment.

You will recall that she (the intellect and the senses) ate of the fruit because she thought it was good (an advantage). When something is judged as an advantage (as good), the emotion of desire accompanies the thought, and when something is judged as a threat (as bad), the emotion of fear accompanies the thought. And so now they have "experienced" (or eaten of) the fruit of the tree of the knowledge of good and of evil.

When he (the man) told the Lord God that he was afraid because he was (or had been) naked, and that he had hidden himself, the Lord God said, "Who told you that you were naked? Have you eaten of the fruit of the tree of the knowledge of good and evil, whereof I commanded you not to eat?"

Shifting the Blame

And the man (the mind) said, "The woman (the intellect and the senses), whom you gave to be with me, she gave it to me, and I ate it." He was actually blaming the Lord God when he said "the woman whom *you* gave to be with me." Then the Lord God asked the woman (the intellect and the senses) what she had done. And she said, "The serpent (the sense of separation) beguiled me, and I ate the fruit." These, obviously, are the first examples of "shifting the blame."

The Serpent Is Cursed Above All Cattle

The Lord God said to the serpent, "Because you have done this, you are cursed above all cattle." The meaning of "cursed" is "calamitous and abominable misfortune." And the original meaning of the word "cattle" is "personal property" (that which we own). The Lord God was saying to the serpent that the most "cursed" (calamitous and abominable misfortune) of all that we "own" (claim to be ours) is the belief of separateness or apartness.

We can see that all the thoughts and emotions involved with our acceptance or "ownership" of the "belief" that we have a selfhood separate and apart from God have magnified and deepened the patterns made by the electrical currents on our circuit map. These belief patterns have intensified to such a degree that our conviction that we have a separate selfhood is irrefutable.

The Birth of Personal Sense

You will recall that the Lord God admonished them, saying, "You may eat of all the trees of the Garden except the fruit of the tree of the knowledge of good and evil. But if you eat of that tree you will surely die." As you know, the serpent refuted the Lord God's admonition, and he said to the woman (the intellect and the senses), "If you eat of the fruit of the tree of the knowledge of good and evil, you not only won't die, your eyes will be opened and you will be as gods, knowing good and evil."

As you observe, the serpent did not say, "You will be as God." Of course, God, the Source, is pure, unconditioned consciousness, which is unaffected by what we term good and evil. But he said, "You will be as gods, knowing good and evil."

They fell for the serpent's temptation. They ate the fruit of the tree of the knowledge of good and evil — and they did die. That is, they cut themselves off — or separated themselves — from the Source. And so now they have a sense of a selfhood separate and apart from God. This was the birth of personal sense.

Personal sense sets itself up as a god. The name of God is "I," and so you can see that personal sense not only sets itself up as a god, but also appropriates the name of God, and calls itself "I." The personal sense of I is the "god" that knows (or judges) good and evil.

Each encounter and each situation must now be evaluated according to whether it is good or evil. Since they have cut themselves off from the Source, they must earn their living by "the sweat of their brow." What could be greater drudgery or harder work than taking on the exhausting responsibility of evaluating every single experience as good or evil — that is, whether it is an advantage or a threat?

Of course, our conviction that we have a selfhood separate and apart from God is based on a lie. But we accept this lie as the Truth, and therefore, everything in our lives is determined and built on that premise. We have been hypnotized.

The Effect of the Hypnotism

Here is an example that will illustrate the effect of the hypnotism: Someone owns a mansion, and has ten million dollars in the bank and in investments. But he has been hypnotized and told that he has no place to live and no money — even to buy food. What would he do? He probably would sleep on the street, and rummage in the trash baskets, and beg for money to buy a meal. This may seem to be a drastic illustration, but it is mild compared to the abundance, the peace, the joy, the security, the well-being, and the fulfillment from which we have cut ourselves off by our acceptance of the belief that we have a selfhood apart from God.

The Human Experience

Exactly what is the human experience? It is the hypnotic dream that arises out of our acceptance of the belief that we have a selfhood apart from God, the Source, and that this separate selfhood or personal sense is who we really are. And all this time, our True Identity has been intact — at one with the Source.

The hypnotic beliefs and convictions that we are separate and apart from God — and from All That Is — constitute the human scene. Humanhood is made up of the good and the bad. And as human beings, we are constantly judging what and who is an advantage or a threat to us. Thus we must appropriate, achieve, acquire, defend, and protect ourselves, and fight for survival.

The Universal Hypnotism
or the
Universal Mesmerism

These hypnotic beliefs and convictions not only have been accepted by us, but by all mankind as well. This predicament is not just ours — it is universal. And since this is a "universal" belief of separateness or apartness from God and from each other, we are susceptible to the theories, superstitions, and false beliefs that are accepted by all mankind.

The composite of all these false beliefs, theories, and superstitions forms a "waveband" or "frequency," which acts like a station on the radio that is constantly broad-casting. And because of our acceptance of these beliefs, we are automatically attuned to that frequency, and we are vulnerable and subliminally susceptible to all that is being broadcast. We refer to this waveband or frequency as "the universal hypnotism" or "the universal mesmerism."

The universal mesmerism or universal hypnotism casts a "spell," or a "sleep," which allows the personal self or personal sense to carry out the "hoax" that there is a "selfhood" separate from God (the Source). And as long as the hypnotism continues, there is no possible way to convince the personal self or personal sense that it is simply acting out a charade — "the human scene."

There is a story that I heard several years ago that is a perfect illustration of how the hypnotism works. An experiment was being performed in which a student at a university was hypnotized and told that he had been to the Kentucky Derby. While he was hypnotized, he was asked a question about where he had been that day. And he replied that he had been to the Kentucky Derby. Then they said to him, "You couldn't have been there, because you were in school." And he said, "Well, I was in school in the morning, but I flew down to the Kentucky Derby in the afternoon." And they said, "You couldn't possibly have been there because this isn't even the time of the year for the Kentucky Derby." He said, "Oh yes, I was there. They had an extra Kentucky Derby."

The hypnotic spell comes as a complete package. The "victim" is acting out a hoax, but nevertheless, every aspect of the experience is solidly based on the assumption that what is believed is the Truth.

In the human scene, we are governed by the intellect and the senses — which deal only with the outer. But our oneness with the Spirit or the Source is our true state and our True Identity. And It has not changed throughout this hypnotic spell, which is produced by the illusion of separateness.

How to Break the Hypnotic Spell

As you know, the first chapter of Genesis ends with: "And God saw everything He had made, and behold, it was very good." This was the Spiritual Universe — "a state of oneness" and pure bliss.

The human scene is "a state of separateness" — a hypnotic spell — perpetuated by the constant focus of the attention on judging good and evil.

In Joel Goldsmith's book, *The Infinite Way,* one of the "Wisdoms" is, "God is not in the human scene." What a shock it was for me, when I read that statement! So what is the answer? How can we "break" the hypnotic spell of the human scene? We must be still, and enter the realm where God is — the Kingdom Within.

What is it that must be still? It is the intellect and the senses. The intellect and the senses deal only with the outer — that which has already been formed. They are a part of the mind, but they have no contact with the Spirit. We do not condemn the intellect and the senses, however, because their purpose is to allow us to experience that which is being formed. But we do not permit ourselves to be governed by them.

When the intellect and the senses are still, and the attention of the mind is turned inward, we are governed by the Spirit. And the pure Invisible Spiritual Energy flows forth as unconditioned form and experience. We do not "still" the mind — we "still" the intellect and the senses. We still all the activity that deals with the outer — with that which has already been formed.

When the attention of the mind is turned inward toward the Source, and the intellect and the senses are still, the activity that deals with the outer ceases, and we can "turn within." We call this meditation. The mind (the instrument or avenue of awareness) is centered on the Source — the state of consciousness of unconditioned bliss. The sense of separation no longer exists — the hypnotism is broken — and an "experience of oneness" is reestablished. As the mind rests there — with the attention turned toward the Spirit — what happens? We are letting the Spirit "take over" and flow forth pure, fresh, and unconditioned — forming all things new. This is how things change. This is how healings take place.

When the intellect and the senses are still, and the attention of the mind is centered within, we may have a conscious "experience of oneness" with the Source. We may experience a "feeling" of peace; or we may experience the "Silence." Or we may receive impartations from the

Spirit. Or the experience may come as the fulfillment of our needs. But we don't hold a vessel, or a container, waiting for something that we expect or hope will come forth and fill our order. We rest here in "the Now." And we "let."

Who We Really Are: Our True Identity

Because, as human beings, we have accepted as the truth the belief that we are separate and apart from God, we have reacted by constantly searching for God. We have been on a long, long journey. And where has God been all this time? Within! We have sought and searched everywhere. Yet, all the time we have been told that "The Kingdom of God is Within" — Within Our Own Being.

What does "Within — Within Our Own Being" mean? Why is this so difficult to understand? It not only is difficult, it is impossible, because we are trying to understand the Spirit with the intellect. And, of course, since the intellect deals only with the "outer," it cannot comprehend "the things of the Spirit."

So what *should* we do? "Be still, and *know* that 'I' am God." The name of God is "I." This does not mean, however, that I, the personal sense of I — Lorene, or Mary, or John — am God. It means that the "I that I am," the Infinite Invisible Spiritual Energy or the Life Force at the Center of My Very Own Being, is God. The "I that I am" is One with the Source.

Be still, and let well up from within you the name of God, "I." Do not speak the name of God, "I," but deep within, let the name "I" silently and gently voice Itself: "I.". . "I.". . "I.". . . . This is your name — at the Center of Your Very Own Being.

Jesus said, "I and my Father are One." The word "Father" puzzled and confused me because I always thought of the word "father" in relation to a male parent. But then I understood that Jesus was using the word "Father" to mean "God" or the "Source." And I realized that when He said, "I and my Father are One," He was not referring to the personal sense of I, but to the "I" at the Center of His Being. He made this very clear, when He said, "I of myself can do nothing, but the Father within, He doeth the work."

When Jesus said, "I and my Father are One," He was consciously aware of His Oneness with the Father. He didn't mean, however, that only He, Jesus, and the Father are One. The "I" that Jesus was speaking of when He said, "I and my Father are One," is the same "I" that is at the Center of My Being, and the same "I" that is at the Center of Your Being. This "I" is "closer than breathing and nearer than hands and feet." This is already true — and has always been true — whether we are aware of it or not. So we, too, can say, "I and my Father (God — the Source) are One."

"God is where God is realized" is one of the principles of The Infinite Way. And even though we say, "I and my Father are One," it means nothing until we — ourselves — have a conscious realization of this Truth.

"Ye shall know the Truth, and the Truth shall make you free." Therefore, "Be still and know that I am God," means that we become still enough to consciously realize that the "I that I am" (at the Center of My Being) is God (the Source).

Jesus not only said, "I and my Father are One," but He also said, "All that the Father hath is mine." And He said, "Take no thought for your life — what you shall eat, or what you shall drink, or wherewithal you shall be clothed. It is the Father's good pleasure to give you the Kingdom." This means that, when I am conscious of my oneness with God (the Source), I can be still and allow this pure, unconditioned, Infinite Invisible Spiritual Energy, which "I" am — at the Center of My Being — to flow forth as love, peace, joy, abundance, well-being, and the fulfillment of every need. I don't have to ask it. I don't have to tell it. All that is required is my attention, awareness, and recognition, as I abide in the Stillness — "The Secret Place of the Most High."

And this "I" that is within is forever saying: "I will never leave you nor forsake you." "I am the bread, the meat, the wine, the water." "I in the midst of thee am mighty." "I go before thee to make the crooked places straight."

Experiencing Oneness

We can understand how the experiences of separateness or apartness and judging good and evil cut us off not only from our neighbor, but also from the Source, which is at the Center of Our Very Own Being. And we've discovered that the secret is being still — turning away from the outer — and giving our attention to the Source within. But how can we manage to do that all the time, and live in "this world"?

If there is someone who is giving us a hard time, someone we are condemning, or an enemy of any kind, we know what is happening. Isn't the intellect just talking all the time — shifting and turning and keeping everything stirred up? Have you ever listened to yourself — talking inside yourself? We're just "telling them off!" The intellect not only is talking, but it is being fueled by the emotions — "heating up" the situation — and further intensifying, solidifying, and perpetuating the belief of separation.

So how do we deal with this? What is the answer? The answer is consciously reestablishing and maintaining an "experience of oneness." And this is the purpose of forgiveness, non-judgment, and non-condemnation.

And now, we can see why Jesus said: "Thou shalt love the Lord thy God, with all thy heart, with all thy soul, and with all thy mind. This is the first and greatest commandment." Then He said, "And the second is like unto it. Thou shalt love thy neighbor as thyself." Of course, He was telling us to have an "experience of oneness" with the Source, which is God, at the Center of Our Own Being, and to have an "experience of oneness" with our neighbor — and with All That Is — as ourself.

A basic principle of The Infinite Way is, "God constitutes individual Being." And another basic principle is, "My conscious oneness with God constitutes my oneness with all Spiritual Being and Idea." That is, my conscious oneness with God (The Infinite Invisible Source) — which constitutes My Being — constitutes my oneness with the Spiritual Being and Nature of everyone and everything (with All That Is) in the entire Universe.

Once, after a class and a visit with Joel and Emma in Hawaii, I was returning home to New York. We were flying over the Pacific, and as I sat by the window, looking down at the ocean, I glanced at my foot. And the thought and feeling swept over me: "The ocean is as much a part of me as my foot! This is myself." I frequently remember this as a profound example of an "experience of oneness."

When I am consciously aware of my oneness with the Source at the Center of My Being, I can have an "experience of oneness" with All That Is: With the Being of every individual, with every plant, flower, tree, and every blade of grass, with every bird and animal, with every stone and mineral on this planet, with the oceans, the earth and the sky, with the entire Universe, with all the galaxies — even the farthest star.

Do you now more fully understand that we condemn only that from which we feel separate or apart? If we have an "experience of oneness," there will be no occasion to condemn or judge good and evil. But, of course, until we have attained a perpetual "experience of oneness," there must be continual forgiveness, non-condemnation, and non-judgment.

A Contemplative Meditation

Now let's have an experience of going back into the Garden of Eden. I suggest that you read the following section in a meditative state, and then close your eyes, and recalling what you read, "turn within" and go through the experience again. As you know, when we say we are "turning within," we mean that we are turning away from the outer, and centering our attention on the Source Within Our Own Being. You may think of the following as a contemplative meditation:

I know that the Garden of Eden is a state of consciousness — pure spiritual bliss. I'm leaving all form, I'm leaving all concepts, opinions, and judgments. I'm centering the mind on The Infinite Invisible Source Within My Own Being. And I am returning to the state of unconditioned consciousness — the state of "Is."

I recall the Bible passage, "As I was with Thee before the world was," before form was, before effect was. I am entering into the state of consciousness of unconditioned bliss. And I am resting here in "the Now." The "I that I am" is "at one" with the Source — at the Center of My Being.

Omnipresence. . .Omnipotence. . .Omniscience. . .
Pure and Unconditioned Infinite Invisible Spiritual
Energy. . .Limitless, Unfathomable, and All-
Encompassing — right here where I am resting —
in "the Now". . .I'm not restricting it. . . I'm not
holding it back. . .I am abiding in an Infinite Ocean
of Omnipresence.

Omnipotence. . .An Infinite Ocean of Omnipotence
. . .The All-and-Only Power — Infinite and
Unconditioned. . .No fear. . .No resistance. . .No
desire. . .Just an experience of "Is" and "Now."

An Infinite Ocean of Unconditioned Omniscience. . .
All-Wisdom. . .All-Knowingness. . .Indescribable. . .
Unimaginable. . .The intellect does not need to grab
hold of even a Truth. . .I relax and rest in an Infinite
Ocean of Unconditioned Omniscience.

I rest here — in "the Now" — and I allow
Omnipresence, Omnipotence, Omniscience to flow
forth as pure unconditioned form. I don't have a list
of requests that I am expecting It to fill. I don't have
to ask It. I don't have to direct It. Omniscience does
not need instruction. I let It flow forth while I give
my attention to this pure state of Unconditioned Bliss.

Omnipresence, Omnipotence, Omniscience. This,
we call God. There is only God . . . IT is all there is
. . . IT constitutes my Being. ITS name is "I." There
is no "me" requiring somebody or something that

appears to be separate to fulfill "me." As I abide here in "the Now," the "I that I am" fulfills Itself as an "experience of oneness" with God (the Source) and with my neighbor — and with All That Is — as myself.

I am beginning to experience a peace that is beyond understanding. Are there enemies here? Are there problems here? If an enemy or a problem remains, it is only a temptation for me to judge someone or something as being separate — a temptation to accept a presence or a power other than God, the Source, at the Center of My Being. Here, where "I am," is the point at which the Infinite Invisible Spiritual Energy — pure and unconditioned — is flowing forth.

And now, with your eyes closed, and in a meditative state, let flow over you the experience that you have just had. You do not need to try to recall any of the words — but if they come, embrace them. Abide and rest here in "the Now" as long as you wish.

When we have such an experience as this, it all seems clear and obvious. But when we go back into our daily activities, we find that constant reminders and practice are essential to allow this change to continue to take place in our consciousness. Forgiveness, non-condemnation, and non-judgment are our part. The Spirit does the rest.

Living Humanly and Living Spiritually

Do you see that we are arriving at a new experience, where we live not by that which comes to us — but by that which flows out through us and from us? When we live humanly, we are constantly looking outside for "the good" to come to us, or we are protecting or defending ourselves from "the evil" that may be out there.

When we live humanly, as "man of earth," we are always expecting something to come toward us from the outside. But when we live spiritually, as "man who has his Being in Christ," we live from the center outward: "I" give, "I" forgive, "I" bestow.

To illustrate "living spiritually," you can visualize, or actually draw, a circle with arrows pointing outward (from the circle). And to illustrate "living humanly," you can visualize, or draw, a circle with arrows pointing inward (toward the circle).

When we live humanly, we are not aware that God (the Source) is within us, but we think that God is outside — separate from us. As human beings, we live by the good and the bad. It is no wonder that the God that was "made" by "man of earth" would be a God of reward and a God of vengeance.

Spiritually, we are not looking outside for a God to bring something to us. We are "at one" with God (The Infinite Invisible Source). And all our needs are met, as love, forgiveness, healing, and whatever it is that is spiritual, flow out through us to the world.

Living humanly is perpetually "experiencing separateness." Living spiritually is perpetually "experiencing oneness." When we are making the transition from living humanly to living spiritually, it is forgiveness, non-condemnation, and non-judgment that bring us out of "an experience of separateness" into "an experience of oneness."

We began with "Love greets you." Love — "an experience of oneness" — lifts up that which has been "bent." Living spiritually is living "upright." When we live humanly, we live "horizontally," "bowed down" and crawling back and forth from the past to the future — but never in the present. When we live spiritually, we live in the uprightness of "the Now" — in the perpendicular split second of the present moment.

Earlier, we digressed from the emphasis on the theme of an "experience of oneness" so that we could go back to the Garden of Eden, in Genesis, and determine the nature of an "experience of separateness" and how it took place. We must remember, however, that the temptation to "experience separateness" and the opportunity to "experience oneness" happen all day long, every day.

Now, we understand that the "experience of separateness or apartness" and judging good and evil cut us off not only from our neighbor but also from the Source — the Spirit of God Within Our Own Being. When we speak of "cutting ourselves off from the Source," we should remember that this means that we are "cutting ourselves off" from the Infinite, Invisible Spiritual Energy, which is the Life Force that flows through us and manifests as us. When we cut ourselves off from the Source, we are "on our own."

There is a Bible passage that is a corroboration of the preceding explanation. "If you abide in Me (the Spirit — the Source) and let Me abide in you, you will bear fruit richly. But if you do not abide in Me and let Me abide in you, you will be as a branch that is cut off and withereth."

We can now see even more clearly why Jesus said, "Love (have an experience of oneness with) the Lord, thy God," and "Love (have an experience of oneness with) thy neighbor as thyself."

When I refuse to forgive, or when I condemn or judge someone for something they did or didn't do, I am "experiencing separateness." But when I forgive them, or release them from my condemnation and judgment — or if I "catch myself" in time to refuse to condemn or judge — I am "experiencing oneness." I am loving my neighbor as myself. My neighbor is myself. We have the same name, "I," at the Center of Our Being.

Now, of course, it becomes even more obvious why forgiveness, non-condemnation, and non-judgment provide the key for breaking the hypnotic spell of the human scene.

The Value of Working With the Lists

By this time, we should be more sensitive and more aware of what is going on within us. I can tell you that those who have worked with the lists — and with all the suggestions that have been given so far — have actually transformed not only their own lives, but also the lives of many of those around them whom they had formerly condemned.

You may feel that working in this way couldn't possibly affect those we've formerly condemned, and have now released into their Christhood — but it does. And even though the work that we do is never in an effort to "change" anyone, the change that takes place in our consciousness often affects others to such a degree that many times they do change. Those who have worked with these suggestions — with dedication — have witnessed what they consider to be "miracles."

Each of the three following sections contains an example of an experience of a student who has worked diligently with the suggestions given so far in this book.

What to Do if
Somebody Won't Even Speak to You

One of the students worked in an advertising agency. He was an artist, and he worked in a large area (called the "bull pen") where many other artists and graphic designers had their desks. There was another artist who had his desk right next to the desk of the student. And for some reason, the man was angry with the student and wouldn't speak to him. The student never knew what was the matter, but the man simply would not speak.

This developed into a perfectly horrible experience for the student. Furthermore, everybody in the bull pen knew that this awkward situation existed between the two of them. The student was so upset that he couldn't do his work. He was becoming such a nervous wreck that he just couldn't do anything at all.

So I agreed to give him help in dealing with this predicament. But I began by saying, "You know that you can't try to change the man. Don't try to change him or get him to speak to you. I can't help you with that. But just work with the steps of the Procedure for Forgiveness." He already knew that he should begin by turning away from the situation and asking himself: "What have I ever done that I wish I hadn't done?" or, "What haven't I done that I wish I had done?"

Of course, what he chose to think of did not need to have anything to do with the present situation. Then he proceeded to ask himself, "What made me do it?" Or, "Why didn't I do it?" And he followed through with all the steps of the Procedure for Forgiveness — many times each day.

He kept working in this way, and finally, one day, the man did speak to him. Then the other artists said, "Well, we see that you and so-and-so are finally speaking to each other!" And the student, with anger, blurted out, "What's that to you!" Of course, then he not only had to forgive everybody in the bull pen, but he, himself, had to be forgiven for losing his temper. He continued the forgiveness work, and some time later he was offered a much better job as the art director of another company.

Often he would make an appointment to see me during his lunch hour, and many times, he would say, "I can't come on that day, because I'm having lunch with my friend." His "friend" was the man who wouldn't speak to him at the place where he previously worked. They had become the closest of friends. And the only contact the student had at the place where he had worked before was with this particular man.

This is the kind of thing that often happens when we do this work. It looks as if it is the outer picture that changes. And it does. But it changes because our own consciousness has changed. When consciousness changes, the form and the experience change. This student was lifted out of the kind of work that he was doing into a whole new experience. And in addition, he acquired a wonderful new friend.

The Stolen Purse

There is something else in relation to the application of these principles that I want to tell you. It's about a girl whose purse was stolen. She called me for help, and I said, "I can't help you find the purse, but I'll work with you. Of course, you know that you must begin by forgiving whoever it was who took the purse. I know this is going to be difficult, but I'll help you."

So we worked together. Immediately, she turned away from the one who had taken the purse, and asked herself, "Have I never done anything that I wish I hadn't done?" She followed through with all the steps of the Procedure for Forgiveness — withdrawing her condemnation, and finally, releasing the individual into his or her Christhood or True Identity.

A few days later, she said, "I actually feel love for that person — whoever it is." You see, her attention was no longer on finding the purse. But she continued to work in the same way. And after a few more days, the purse was found. It had been placed in a washroom in another building that was owned by the company where she worked. Everything was intact except the money, which her company replaced.

Now what is really important is that her consciousness had totally changed during this intense experience of working with the steps of the Procedure for Forgiveness.

At the time her purse was stolen, she was living in a very unsatisfactory and uncomfortable apartment. But after our work together with the Procedure for Forgiveness, "out of the blue" she was offered a beautiful home in the country, with a garden, a grand piano, and more luxuries than she could have ever dreamed of. The experience had changed her consciousness to the degree that she could no longer live in the place where she had formerly lived.

I often feel that I shouldn't tell the end of these stories, because then you may think, "If I do it, I might get the reward at the other end." You will recall, however, that when consciousness changes, the form and experience change. This is why we don't need to be concerned about the experience and the form. We need to be concerned only with changing our consciousness.

There is something else that I want to mention in relation to this situation about the stolen purse. When we do this kind of work, we know that there are thousands of others who are tempted to steal purses and things of much greater value. But when we work in this way, we are not "working on" a person. We are not trying to change them. We are dealing only with consciousness — recognizing that whatever they are tempted to do is not of their True Identity, but it is the effect of the universal mesmerism. And we no longer condemn them to their humanhood, but we release them into their Christhood.

When we were working with the situation concerning the purse, I knew that the individual who took the purse had been healed. And I realized also that there were many others who probably were healed at the same time. You see, this work enters a particular stratum. And so if we don't "aim it" at somebody, it can enter consciousness, and be available for all those who are receptive.

The Chest of Silver

I've frequently told about the girl and the stolen purse.
The story is recorded on a tape of a class that I gave.
And I scheduled a class at which I was to play the
particular tape again. There was a couple who wanted
to attend the class, but they were moving into a new
apartment, and some of the things that belonged to the
people who previously lived there were still in the
apartment. The students asked the superintendent of
the building if their things could be moved in during
the afternoon while they were away, and he agreed. So
while they were at the class, the superintendent opened
the apartment to let their things be moved in. When
the students went to the apartment after the class, the
people who had lived there before came back and said,
"Our chest of silver is gone."

The students called me for help, telling me what a
terrible thing had happened. The people who had
delivered their furniture, obviously had taken the chest of
silver. And I said, "Remember the story about the purse."

They asked me to continue to work with them. And
they worked too, using the steps of the Procedure for
Forgiveness. They always began with, "What have I
done that I wish I hadn't done, and what made me do
it?" They knew that the same universal mesmerism that
had functioned in them was functioning in whoever it
was who had taken the chest of silver. And they always
ended by releasing them into their Christhood or True
Identity.

The next day, the students called the company that had delivered their furniture and spoke about what had happened, telling them that a chest of silver was gone. The owner of the company then spoke to the two men who had delivered their furniture. And one of the men said, "Yes, I took it. I don't know what made me do it. But I'll bring it back." Isn't this just what we've been talking about? "I don't know what made me do it."

More Work to Do

Do you wonder what we do now? We will continue to work with our lists of the names of those we've condemned, or are condemning, *for* doing something, and those we've condemned, or are condemning, *for not* doing something. And of course, we will continue to make lists of the things we've done that we wish we hadn't done, and the things we didn't do that we wish we had done.

Later, you will more fully understand that when we withdraw our condemnation and judgment, and release others into their Christhood, we free them to be who they "really are." As we work in this way, our own consciousness changes. And when our consciousness changes, the form and experience change. Then we will attract fewer and fewer difficult situations and relationships. It's as if a magnet has been "demagnetized."

Whatever we see on the television, hear on the radio, read in the newspapers or magazines, or encounter on the Internet is an opportunity for us to monitor ourselves and observe our reaction.

It is important to remember that we, ourselves, must be forgiven, and that we can be forgiven only as we establish an "experience of oneness" — a conscious feeling of connectedness — with each individual that we condemn. We can't just take care of everyone by issuing a "blanket coverage."

We should ask ourselves whether, by any chance, we have been, or are, condemning certain animals, birds, plants, or insects. When we observe ourselves engaging in such condemnation, we should immediately withdraw our condemnation and judgment, and release the particular animal, bird, plant, or insect into its True Identity.

Do you begin to see more clearly the expanse and the scope of the work we are doing? And are you aware of the responsibility we have?

Working With the Lists as We Use All the Steps of the Procedure for Forgiveness

Now we are ready to return to the Procedure for Forgiveness and work with the lists. You may be thinking, "Oh, no! Not again! We've already done that." But have we given our utmost to this opportunity? Did you really write the lists as we suggested earlier? Someone said to me, "Oh, I have it all in my head. I don't need to write anything down." But unless we write all the lists and follow all the suggestions (and there are more suggestions to come), we will be depriving ourselves of the immense value of this work.

In this section, we will expand the Procedure for Forgiveness. And we will write the instructions in such a way that you can easily follow each step as you work with your lists. Therefore, you will be able to use this section as a reference.

STEP 1:

Write a heading for each of two categories:

One heading is for a list of the names of those you've condemned, or are condemning, "for doing something," and the other heading is for a list of the names of those you've condemned, or are condemning, "for not doing something." Use a separate sheet of paper for each heading, and leave plenty of room below each heading to write lots of names:

(1) **For something they did, or are doing**, and

(2) **For something they didn't do, or aren't doing**.

Now write as many names as you can recall, placing each name under the proper heading. If the same name will fit under each of the two headings, write the name in both places. As you know, it isn't necessary to write what they did or didn't do — the name is sufficient.

There will be many whose names you can't remember, and others whose names you never knew. But you can always find some way of identifying them on the lists.

When you are making your lists, you may find it helpful to write subheadings under each of the main headings. The use of subheadings helps us to focus on particular areas that we might otherwise overlook.

One man told me that he had a whole "book" full of names from his army days. And someone else said that he had a remarkable list from the time he was in elementary school.

You may use some of the following suggestions as examples of subheadings. Or, as you are making your lists, you may wish to simply refer to the suggestions as reminders: Early childhood; Family; Elementary school; High school; College; Father; Mother; Brothers (if any); Sisters (if any); Husband (or ex-Husbands); Wife (or ex-Wives); In-laws; Relatives; Boy friends; Girl friends; Teachers; Students; Doctors; Politicians; Foreign Leaders; Heads of Organizations; Co-workers; Bosses; Employees; Clients; Landlords; Tenants; Neighbors; Workmen; Salespeople; Telephone solicitors; Mail solicitors; Drivers; and on and on. Of course, you may think of examples of your own.

Write as many names as you can think of now, and remain alert, and add more names as they present themselves.

STEP 2:

The next step of the Procedure consists of writing lists of things you've done that you wish you hadn't done, and things you didn't do that you wish you had done.

Write a heading for each of the two categories — using a separate sheet of paper for each heading:

(1) **Things I've done that I wish I hadn't done**, and

(2) **Things I didn't do that I wish I had done**.

Under the first heading, write as many things as you can think of that you've done that you wish you hadn't done, and under the second heading, write as many things as you can think of that you didn't do that you wish you had done. You may find that you can think of more things to write this time than when we first suggested that you make the lists. Don't just "think of things," write them down — briefly — but specifically. (I strongly suggest that you do not leave your lists where anyone will discover them.)

I find it helpful to "go back over the day" each evening before I go to bed — just to be sure that I haven't left anything out, and that I haven't forgotten the things I need to be forgiven for. I also find it a good idea to pause often at different times during the day to check on myself.

STEP 3:

And now look at the name of someone on the list of

those you have condemned, or are condemning, *for doing something*. Don't dwell on the name or the person, and don't rehearse the situation in detail. Instead, turn your attention away from them immediately, and look at something on the list of *things you've done* that you wish you hadn't done, and choose one specific thing. What you choose from your list does not need to relate to the person you are condemning, and neither does it need to be the same kind of thing.

Incidentally, when you have chosen the name of someone from the list of those you've condemned, or are condemning, for doing something, it is easy to get tangled up and choose something from your list of things you didn't do that you wish you had done. For this step, however, you should be sure to choose something from your list of things you've done that you wish you hadn't done.

Now ask yourself, "What made me do that?" You may say, "I don't know why I did it. I wish I hadn't done it — something just took over." Or you may say, "How could I have done that? I can't believe I did it."

Do you see that the person you have been condemning probably could say the same thing? They may feel that something just took over in them too. And they may wonder how they could have done what they did. It now becomes clearer that it was a sense of a "selfhood apart" that was functioning in both of us. It was not the "I that I am" in either of us.

STEP 4:

Now choose someone from the list of those you've condemned, or are condemning, *for not doing* something, and choose something from your list of things you *didn't do* that you wish you had done.

And now ask yourself, "Why didn't I do that? I wish I had done it. Why did I refuse or neglect to do that, when I had the opportunity? It's too late now." When I don't do something that I wish later that I had done, I can see that, at the time, I was just being stubborn, thoughtless, careless, self-centered, or afraid.

So when I get upset and blame or condemn someone for not doing something that I was depending on them to do, I realize that the same thing was functioning in them that was functioning in me when I didn't do something I was expected to do.

I am now able to recognize that the same Spirit that dwells at the Center of My Being dwells at the Center of the Being of the one I have condemned, or am condemning. Even though we seem to be separate, we are One. We are One with the Source and One with each other. But unless I realize this Truth, it is impossible to have an experience of oneness — a conscious feeling of connectedness — with the one I've been condemning.

STEP 5:

When you are working with someone whose name is on the list, you may feel that you want to reach out for their hand — not to shake hands with them, or to look at them, but just to reach out to the side for their hand in loving recognition of the oneness. Then you can say, deep inside, "I no longer condemn you or judge you. With love (an experience of oneness), the 'I that I am' releases you into your Christhood — your True Identity."

Use the five steps of the Procedure for Forgiveness as you look at each name on the list of those you've condemned for doing something — referring to your own list of things you have done that you wish you hadn't done.

And now use the steps of the Procedure for Forgiveness as you look at each name on the list of those you've condemned for not doing something — referring to the things you didn't do that you wish you had done. Each time we work with the lists, we should remember that we can be forgiven only as we forgive.

The Infinite Way principle, "God constitutes individual Being," is one that I constantly carry in my awareness. It contains a secret of spiritual living. As I no longer condemn or judge an individual, but allow the "I that I am" to release him or her into their Christhood, I am recognizing that God constitutes their Being — their True Identity.

When we arrive at the final step of the Procedure for Forgiveness, we should look at each name on the lists of those we have condemned and say and "feel" deep within, "I withdraw my condemnation and judgment, and with love (an experience of oneness), the 'I that I am' releases you into your Christhood — your True Identity. God constitutes Your Being, and God constitutes My Being."

More About Personal Sense

You will recall that we talked about the fact that we never could remember very many things that we had done or hadn't done that we could put on our lists. This indicates something very important — but very subtle. It is this: There is something that "shuts off" in us and will not let us see what we have done or haven't done. We really don't see it. This is personal sense. This is the way personal sense works. Personal sense is protecting itself, and so it does not allow us to see what it does not want us to see.

When we were discussing the Garden of Eden, we found that personal sense is a sense of a separate self-hood. And so personal sense tries to maintain that separateness — because otherwise, it cannot exist.

Personal sense knows that every time there is an "experience of oneness" with my neighbor, there is, at the same time, an "experience of oneness" with the Source. And every time that happens, personal sense knows that it has to go, because personal sense is only where separateness is. Do you see that? Where there is oneness, there is no personal sense.

Once, a student asked the question, "How can we tell whether it is the Spirit or personal sense?" It is very easy to tell which I is speaking, because the personal sense of I always wants it for "me," or it wants to defend or protect "me." The personal sense of I is always trying to acquire, appropriate, achieve, defend, and protect itself. And it condemns anything or anyone that confronts it or interferes with it. But the "I that I am," at the Center of My Being, gives, forgives, blesses, and heals.

The Personal Sense of I Cannot Forgive

One of the most important points in the entire book is this: *The personal sense of I cannot forgive.* The personal sense of I is the separate selfhood that judges good and evil. Only the "I that I am" can forgive. When Jesus said, "Father forgive them," He was speaking of the "I that I am" at the Center of His Being. And this is the only "I" that can forgive. When the personal sense of I says, "I forgive you," it means nothing.

Have you followed the suggestions that were given in each of the five steps of the Procedure for Forgiveness? Are you tempted to keep on reading to see what comes next? Or are you thinking, "Maybe I'll do that later, but not yet. I really don't want to do this, anyway." This is an opportunity that we cannot afford to miss. So, work with each individual on your lists — and go as deeply as you can.

When you were working with the lists, did you, by any chance, think of someone you have been condemning for a long, long time, and you felt that you wanted to tell them you have forgiven them for what they did? For heaven's sake, don't do that! You will only create an awkward, embarrassing, and uncomfortable situation. And the individual may not even know (or remember) what you are talking about. Forgiving is something that happens in our own consciousness, and it is the way in which we, ourselves, are forgiven. Our own change of consciousness should be our concern.

Turn It Loose

When a situation arises that involves condemnation, have you ever found that you simply can't, or won't, turn it loose? We keep holding on to it, and rehearsing it and going over and over and over it instead of just dropping it instantly, and using the steps of the Procedure for Forgiveness. In relation to "turning it loose," there are two examples that I use as illustrations.

One example is found in the Old Testament. We are told that outside the Temple there was a brazier upon which they had to put a live sacrifice before they could enter. When something comes up that offends us, or when we feel condemnation or resentment toward somebody, we must be willing to turn it loose immediately and "throw it on the brazier" while it is still "alive and kicking." Otherwise, we will not be able to enter the "Temple of Oneness Within Our Own Being."

The other example is a well-known story about two monks who had been on a journey, and were returning to the monastery. They came to a stream, where a beautiful maiden was trying to get across. One of the monks picked her up and carried her across the stream and set her down on the other side, and they went on their way. Toward sunset, they were turning into the monastery, and the monk who hadn't picked up the maiden said to the other monk, "Now you know perfectly well that you shouldn't have done that. It was a terrible thing that you did. You know that we are not even supposed to look at a woman let alone pick one up, and carry her across the stream." And the other monk said, "Have you been carrying her all day? I left her at the stream."

These two examples illustrate an important aspect of our work. There is something that I frequently do that helps me to quickly "throw it on the brazier" or "leave it at the stream." If I find myself feeling annoyed, or if I catch myself judging, condemning, or complaining, then and there (if I remember in time), I simply say to myself, "Have I ever done anything I shouldn't have done?" Or, if I'm judging or condemning someone for not doing something, I say, "Have I always done what I should have done?" Or, even more briefly, I say, "Have I always been so perfect?" And it stops the judgment or condemnation instantly, and cuts it right off. It "reverses the props." This is an expression I learned years ago when I was taking flying lessons. To stop the plane, we reversed the propellers, which we referred to as "reversing the props."

Condemnation Attracts More of Its Kind

I must say, however, that I have not always been so alert. One Saturday morning, when I was about to give a weekend class in my apartment, I got ready to have my breakfast, and I put a slice of bread in the toaster. By the time I prepared an egg and coffee, smoke was rising — and my toast was burned to a crisp. Someone had used the toaster and had turned it up as far as it would go — and left it that way. You can imagine how I felt, when students would be coming shortly to the apartment for the class — with the place full of smoke and the smell of burnt toast. I was furious. And all the condemnation I was capable of was silently poured out to whoever it was who had used the toaster.

Then after I tried to "air out" the place, I went downstairs to get the mail. And the lobby was in total disarray. They were doing a yearly cleaning job. My condemnation apparatus was already in full gear. And the cleaners, and everybody connected with the building, all the way back to the management and owners received a full — though silent — blast. I *did* want the place to look nice when the students came!

As if this were not enough, just when it was time for the students to arrive, the doorbell rang, and it was a delivery of flowers that someone had sent. There was too much water in the vase, and the water spilled all over the floor in the foyer. And of course, I had to mop it up. Now wouldn't you think they would know not to put so much water in the vase! Need I say more?

It is obvious that a lot of time and energy can be saved if we catch the judgment or condemnation quickly — before it has time to multiply. Otherwise we are apt to "ruin our day" and maybe more — without realizing what did it. The thought, with its accompanying emotion of judgment or condemnation, switches us onto another channel, and we are then tuned in to all the negativity that operates on that frequency. What begins as a "small" condemnation or judgment can, and will, attract more and more of its kind — until it grows far beyond simply having a "disgruntled day" or walking around carrying a "low-grade grudge."

Cutting Ourselves Off From the Source

It is so easy to forget that even the slightest condemnation or judgment cuts us off from the Source. And the moment we cut ourselves off from the Source, we are, at the same time, issuing an invitation to anything and everything in the human scene that happens to come along. When we understand the price we pay for seemingly insignificant indulgences, we may realize that they are "luxuries" we can no longer afford.

So our real challenge is vigilance. It seems unbelievable that, after hearing all the admonitions — and we honestly feel that we understand and want to practice what we've been told — we find ourselves going right ahead in the same old way! One student told me recently that even in the midst of this practice, he was shocked to discover that "in his head" he was really "raking someone over the coals," and "telling them off."

Of course, this is personal sense — and it is the law of self-preservation at work. We know that when the law of self-preservation is at work, there is a sense of separateness — a "two-ness." If I'm feeling separate from my neighbor, any neighbor, anywhere, then I'm not "at one," and I must realize that personal sense is in charge.

An Experience of Oneness Is the Secret

In the works of Spiritual Masters and the books I've read about their teachings, I have often seen the word "atonement." I always felt sad and uncomfortable when I saw the word, because I thought of it in relation to making amends for past mistakes. And that is the definition in the dictionary. But then it came to me that the word "atonement" actually means "at one-ment." So, atonement, or to be "at one," was further confirmation that love — an "experience of oneness " — *is* the secret.

The goal is to get back into the "experience of oneness," because that is the only way I can be sure that

I'm living spiritually. If not, then I know that I'm living humanly as "man of earth, not under the law of God." As a human being, of course, I am subject to whatever the human scene has to offer.

As a human being, I am all alone — cut off and separate from God, and from my neighbor. At times, I am afraid, distressed, frustrated, and depressed. And underneath, I feel guilty because, down deep, I know that I am responsible. I bring this condition about daily because of my condemnation and judgment, and my lack of forgiveness. The realization that I am the one who is responsible carries with it a feeling of guilt. Where there is guilt, there is punishment. This punishment, which is self-imposed, manifests as "solitary confinement" — a perpetual sense of separation.

So if we are going to live spiritually — at one with the Source, with our neighbor, and with All That Is — we have to constantly observe what we are allowing to go on within us. We can no longer permit ourselves to indulge in criticism, inner talking, blame, suspicion, resistance, frustration, worry, resentment, envy, jealousy, gossiping, judgment, condemnation, lack of forgiveness, or negativity of any kind.

A lot of times, we wear the negative badge of martyr-dom while we "brag" about suffering more than anyone else has ever suffered. Sometimes, we just get mad at the whole world, and everybody and everything in it. All of this that we allow to function in us is usurping the place of the Spirit. When we observe that we are allowing such negative attitudes to take over, we must recognize that we are in our most "extreme humanhood," and that anything is liable to happen to us.

In my humanhood, I am not under the law of God, and neither indeed can be. And therefore, I shouldn't be surprised at what I attract to myself. We know that the human scene is made up of the good and the bad, and so the law of averages will bring some good. But we have no way of knowing what will come next. We just "draw a number," and anything can be on it. Joel once said to me, "As a human being, we are merely a statistic."

Still More About Personal Sense

I realize now that in my metaphysical and spiritual "pursuits," I had always been trying to find something to put on top of that which I already had. That is, personal sense had always been trying to "add to itself." It was like putting the sauce on top of a spoiled pudding. It still was spoiled!

Have you thought about the fact that in our metaphysical and spiritual studies and pursuits, we have been trying to "spiritualize" our human selves? More precisely, we have been trying to get the spiritual benefits to apply to our human experience. Of course, no matter how long or how hard we try, we would never be able to accomplish it. It's just not possible. Do you realize that what we have actually been trying to do all along is to improve our personal selves — our humanhood? In other words, we've been trying to use the Spirit to "add to" personal sense. Is this shocking?

But do you know what has to happen? Personal sense has to go. Personal sense has "to die" — so that we can be reborn of the Spirit. The Apostle Paul said, "Die daily." Do you now see what he meant? And do you know how this takes place? Every time we consciously establish an "experience of oneness" with the Source, or with our neighbor, personal sense dies — it disappears. Because it can exist only where there is "separateness." Personal sense cannot experience oneness.

The students all say, "This is very hard!" It is! I agree. But do we have a choice? Jesus knew that it was difficult. And John knew that it was difficult.

In John's First General Epistle, he said, "I bring you no new commandment. I give you an old commandment, which you have heard from the beginning: Love one another. Love one another." And at the very end of His ministry, almost the last thing Jesus said to His disciples was, "Love one another." And what is love? Love is an "experience of oneness."

Someone once remarked to a great man that it was too bad that Christianity hadn't worked. And the man's reply was: "It's never been tried." Jesus said, "The way is straight and narrow, and few there be that enter." If anybody is going to enter — why not us? We are now being given a way —"a new way to live."

Working with the lists provides the key that enables us to make the transition from living humanly to living spiritually. We should take the names on the lists one at a time, and go through the steps of the entire Procedure for Forgiveness — finally releasing each individual into his or her Christhood, or True Identity. When we release an individual into his or her Christhood, we are no longer condemning them to their humanhood, but we are recognizing their True Identity, and that God constitutes their Being. They go free and we go free. When we say or think, "You go free and I go free," it may seem that we are saying, "You go your way, and I go mine," thereby again setting up an "experience of separateness." But we always can tell whether we really have arrived at an "experience of oneness."

Shifting the Blame

We have discussed various ways that we condemn. But there is a very important one that we haven't talked about in relation to ourselves — and it is "shifting the blame." Earlier, in the section concerning the Garden of Eden, we mentioned that perhaps the first example of "shifting the blame" occurred when the man blamed his wife for giving him the fruit of the tree of the knowledge of good and evil — which he ate. And she, in turn, blamed the serpent for beguiling her, and tempting her to eat the fruit.

When we feel guilty, or when something goes wrong, have you ever noticed that we instantly shift the blame to someone or something else?

I've thought a lot about the phenomenon of "shifting the blame," and I've wondered why it is so hard to take the responsibility when we make a mistake or when we do something wrong. When we know that it is "our fault," we automatically feel a flash of guilt. But personal sense instantly diverts our attention by blaming something or someone else — thus protecting and defending itself.

There is absolutely no logic involved, and often the object of our blame is absurd and "far-fetched." For example, we might tear our coat sleeve on a nail and blame the nail and whoever put it there. Or we may have forgotten or neglected to do something we promised to do, and we immediately blame someone else. And if we have a tendency to procrastinate, we can find lots of "legitimate" reasons for shifting the blame. Nevertheless, deluded as we may be, we feel momentarily — though uncomfortably — secure, and relieved of the responsibility for our own carelessness, thoughtlessness, forgetfulness, or neglect. Of course, our anger, guilt, and condemnation have shifted from ourselves to the object or the individual we are blaming.

Do you realize how much time and negative emotional energy can be saved if we catch ourselves immediately, and say or think, "Uh oh! That was my fault," or "I made a mistake." And do it quickly — do it instantly. It is a marvelous, freeing experience. It releases the entire situation. And the very act itself is "spiritually therapeutic."

I have a personal story about "shifting the blame." My Mother always wanted me to sing, and I resented the fact that she constantly brought up the subject — when I didn't want to sing at all. However, when I was in college, although I majored in piano, I took voice lessons as well. My voice teacher wanted me to sing some of the leading roles in the opera productions, but I refused. And so, as a general rule, except for recitals in college, I sang only when I was sure that no one could hear me. Don't ask me why. I can't explain it.

One time, during a college vacation, I was visiting my parents. They were going some place for a little while, and Mother said, "I put some peas on to cook, please look after the peas." Well, as soon as they backed out of the garage, I went in and sat down at the piano and was singing at the top of my voice — and having a wonderful time. I kept singing and singing, and all of a sudden, I smelled the peas burning! Instantly, what came up like a flash was that it was Mother's fault that the peas were burning, because she always wanted me to sing — and I was singing.

How devious personal sense can get! It was a shock to see this, and furthermore, to actually "catch myself in the act." This experience exposed much more than my shifting the blame for the peas burning. I realized that I had never forgiven Mother for wanting me to sing, and

for constantly "bugging" me about it. I always condemned her for it, and without consciously realizing it,
I had been carrying around those buried feelings of
resentment, which actually resulted in perpetual
condemnation and separation.

It's almost scary to see what goes on in us without
our knowing it — or admitting it. But knowing it and
admitting it are not enough. The major part of the
experience is being aware that when I condemn
someone, I am cutting myself off from the Source, and
that I am then totally connected to the human scene.

The Spirit is constantly pouring forth. But when we
condemn or judge, or refuse to forgive, it's as if we've
stepped on the water hose and cut off the flow.

Living Beyond the Level of My Consciousness

After I graduated from college, I gave several successful
concerts. Many who heard me play urged me to
reconsider my earlier resolve not to follow a career as a
performer. But my mind was made up. I was determined
to teach. First, however, there was something that I felt
I simply had to do.

I had always wanted to go to New York. And soon, I
took a long "dreamed-of" trip. I was having a wonderful
experience in New York, going to concerts, the theatre,
the opera, the ballet, and the museums. This really was

a dream come true, and I wanted to continue to stay on far beyond the time that had been designated for my trip. I was staying in a hotel, and my parents had to send me a check each week not only for my hotel bill, but also for all the tickets I was purchasing. I was accustomed to depending on my parents for money. And although I didn't realize it at the time, I took advantage of being "dependent."

After a while, letters from my parents became more and more disturbing. They felt that I should come home. Often when I received a letter, I would carry it around for several days without opening it, because I didn't want to read what they had to say. I didn't want to be upset. I wanted to be in New York to enjoy all that New York had to offer. But I was feeling disgruntled and uncomfortable — without really facing what was disturbing me. My parents' letters seemed to be the reason I was upset, but the real reason had to do with something else that I didn't immediately understand.

I wrote my parents a letter saying that "they were treating me like a child." Then one day, I began to think about what I had said, "They were treating me like a child." Suddenly, I realized that I was insisting on doing what I wanted to do, but at the same time, I was totally dependent on them for money. I was acting like a child — and I deserved to be treated like one.

I knew that in order to feel free, I would have to earn the money to pay my own bills. We often hear of people "living beyond their means." Now I would say that I was "living beyond the level of my consciousness." I was actually living on my parents' consciousness. It's like "pinning someone else's apples on our tree."

This does not mean, however, that we should not accept a gift from someone. But when it becomes a "way of life," and we discover that we are depending on these so-called "gifts," we are living on someone else's consciousness — not on our own.

When we live beyond the level of our consciousness, we feel uncomfortable and guilty. And we usually blame someone else. What I was supposed to be enjoying was not flowing out from within me, and I found that there was no real joy in what I was experiencing. I was not living spiritually — I was living humanly. The arrows were not pointing outward; they were pointing inward — from the outside.

So I got a job in an art gallery, and I stayed on in New York a while longer without being dependent on my parents for money. I had learned a lesson about consciousness (or at least I thought I had), without knowing what to call it at the time. I had learned that I could not live beyond the level of my consciousness.

While I was working in the art gallery, three artists wanted to paint my portrait, and they did. I especially admired the work of one of the artists — not only his portraits, but also his landscapes and cityscapes. The atmosphere that he was able to capture, I found incredible.

I told him that as soon as I returned to Texas, I would be glad to have an exhibition and promote his work. He was delighted to accept my offer. Of course, I didn't have the remotest idea of how I would go about it, but I had volunteered with great enthusiasm.

One day, soon after I returned to Texas, a truck drove up and the driver began to unload crates of paintings. The crates were all over the lawn. Some of the paintings were quite large, and many had glass and elaborate frames. I don't even like to think about the shock, and what my parents had to say and do! The uproar that followed will not be discussed.

I hadn't learned the lesson I thought I had learned about "living beyond the level of my consciousness." I didn't have a car, and I had to depend on my parents and friends to transport the paintings and help set up the exhibitions. I discovered that there are many ways in which we can "live beyond the level of our consciousness." This was another way. I had agreed to accept responsibility that I was not equipped to fulfill. And therefore, I had to impose on my parents and friends to help me carry out my bold and enthusiastic agreement.

I arranged for the paintings to be exhibited in three cities. There was a lot of publicity and interest, and several paintings were sold. An undue amount of credit was given to me for the success of the exhibitions. It was the consciousness of the others, of course, on whom I had imposed, who made the exhibitions possible. When the exhibitions were completed, the paintings that had not been sold, were placed in their respective crates and returned to the artist.

Situations such as I had brought about produce enormous opportunity for condemnation. And I am sure that, in this case, I was the recipient of the ultimate. In addition to making me aware of how I was living beyond the level of my consciousness, this experience provided me with lots of material for my lists of "things I've done that I wish I hadn't done," and "things I didn't do that I wish I had done."

When Things Don't Work Out as We Planned

I had lots of unique ideas for teaching piano, and I looked forward to teaching. Soon I had several pupils. But my teaching pursuits were quickly diverted, and my attention shifted to another direction.

While I was teaching, I was creating some unusual belts, which I had a boot maker manufacture for me. One of the belts I designed had an attractive pocket on the side. And everybody said, "Are you crazy? Nobody will wear a belt with something sticking out on their hip like that!" When I see the kinds of belts with pockets that so many people wear today, I remember what they had said to me.

Over the protests of my parents, I took samples of different designs of my belts that the boot maker had made up for me, and I went to Dallas to show them to

Neiman Marcus. And, then and there, they gave me an order for them. Later, they began to reorder by the gross. But the boot maker said, "I can't fill such orders. After all, I'm a boot maker." So, rather than pursue the belt business, I just gave up the idea.

But I had learned to knit. And I made several two-piece outfits for myself, using the belts I had already designed and some unusual buttons I devised as accessories for the knitted suits. I, of course, was going to take the knitted suits to Neiman Marcus. I'm sure you can understand the total exasperation of my parents, who thought, "How long can this go on!" I proceeded to take the knitted suits to Neiman Marcus, and I actually showed them to Stanley Marcus in person. He liked them and said that he wanted to buy them to sell in the store, but I would have to go to New York to get them manufactured. I was so elated that I didn't think to ask him where I should go when I arrived in New York, or how I should go about getting the suits manufactured. And he had not told me!

I went home and announced to my parents that I was going to New York to get these suits manufactured. I didn't have the vaguest notion of what I would do — but I was going. This, as I recall, was one of our most major blow-ups.

But I brought my designs to New York. And, since I had not been told what to do — without an appointment, or even a phone call — I took my suitcase right to the front door of Saks Fifth Avenue, and asked to see

the buyer of knitted suits. I thought they might be able
to tell me what to do. It turned out that the buyer was
in Europe.

So I went on down to Altmans (another well-known
department store). The person in charge liked my suits,
and wanted to see them on a model. We found that they
didn't have a model who could fit into them. I was very
skinny, and so I had to model them myself. As it turned
out, a manufacturer was sitting there at the time, and saw
me, and liked my designs. And, on the spot, he offered
to manufacture the complete "line" — as they called it.

There was a lot of excitement about the whole
project. And they began to plan ads for Vogue and
Harpers — featuring my name. I made it clear, when I
talked to my parents on the phone, that, of course, they
could now see that I had been right all along, and that I
was going to be famous!

But there was much delay — and non-communica-
tion. I got more and more frantic. Finally, the manufacturer called and asked me to come to his office, which
was on the forty-somethingth floor of a building in the
garment district on Seventh Avenue.

When I walked into his office, his "greeting" was,
"Isn't it terrible, when you look at these windows, and
think how many people jump out of them!" This was a
foreboding of "something," I felt — to say the least.
But of course he was anticipating how shocked I would
be when he told me the news.

The accessories had turned out to cost more to manufacture (by hand) than it cost to manufacture the knitted suits themselves. And this made the price of each suit prohibitive. So they were abandoning the project.

He handed me a box with my originals and the samples they had made. And I left. I was stunned, but I didn't cry. I remember standing on the street corner, waiting for a bus, thinking, "There must be good in all of this. I don't know what it is. But please, just let me see it."

Many times since then, I've thought about how I was turned away from that direction as I — without knowing it — was being prepared for the other work I have been given to do. When things don't work out as we planned, we rarely realize that one door has to close before another can open.

My Body Is My Neighbor

We know that we shouldn't condemn our neighbor. But are we aware that our "neighbor" means not only an individual but also anything and everything in our experience — including our own body? I don't know why, but I had never looked up the original meaning of the word "neighbor" until I thought of neighbor in relation to the body. I found that the original meaning of neighbor is "a near fellow-dweller." Of course, our body is "a *very* near fellow-dweller." You would think we would always feel "at one" with our body. But, instead of feeling at one with your body, have you, at times, actually felt separate from your body — and helpless — because you seemed to be totally victimized or controlled by it?

Whatever we feel separate from we are apt to condemn. If we have a pain or a concern, it becomes a threat, and without realizing it, we condemn the organ or function of our body from which the pain or concern emanates. We can condemn (or feel separate from) an organ or function in our body — our heart, liver, lungs, kidneys, or a toe, or a tooth, or a hand, or a foot. Have you ever said, or heard someone say, "My back is killing me."?

When this idea of our condemning our bodies occurred to me, I began to ponder the fact that consciousness is present in each atom, molecule, and cell in my body. Each atom, molecule, and cell in my body has its own particular vibration and knowingness of its function. And each atom, molecule, and cell has united with other atoms, molecules, and cells to form my heart, and to form my liver, kidneys, lungs, and my bones, muscles, tendons, ligaments, blood, lymph, skin, and hair. The unique vibration of every organ in my body emanates from the Source — the pure unconditioned consciousness that constitutes My Being.

When I have an "experience of oneness" with each atom, molecule, cell, and organ, my body performs its pure unconditioned function. But when I resist, or condemn — or feel separate from — my body or any of its functions or organs, I shut off the "valve" that lets the Spirit (the Infinite, Invisible Spiritual Energy, which I am) flow forth as pure unconditioned form.

However, if we live "spiritually" in our body — from the Source within — our well-being is assured.

Our well-being is already intact. We can't change or improve on it. But we must realize that we, ourselves, can interrupt or cut off the flow of the Spirit by our resistance, condemnation, and judgment, and by our acceptance of the universal beliefs concerning our physical body.

I find it wonderfully rewarding and liberating to have a conscious "experience of oneness" with a particular organ or function of my body that I may have been condemning. A meditation that I use when I wake up in the morning, and just before I go to sleep at night, and many times throughout the day is: "The 'I that I am' is at one with the Source — the pure Spiritual Energy, which constitutes each atom, molecule, cell, organ, and function of my body. My body is the Temple of the Living God."

Bible Passages and Spiritual Principles

Bible passages and spiritual principles are Truths that come to us from the outside through the intellect. Jesus, Moses, Buddha, and others have gone ahead and experienced these Truths. Now, we have the opportunity to experience them for ourselves.

We read the passages and spiritual principles in a book or we hear someone speak them. Learning the Bible passages and spiritual principles and building a vocabulary of them are an essential part of our spiritual growth and development. But they don't make sense to the intellect — because the intellect does not comprehend the things of the Spirit.

So the intellect brings the Bible passages and spiritual principles to us from the outside, and we place them in the mind, which is an instrument or an avenue of awareness, and we leave them there. The passages and principles, themselves, will not change our consciousness. But when we have placed them in the mind and left them there, we can turn within (that is, turn away from the outer), and give our total attention to the Source — the Spirit at the Center of Our Own Being — and be still. Then the Spirit can touch one of those passages or principles — and "light it up." And in the instant that it ignites, it is the Truth for us. "Ye shall know the Truth, and the Truth shall make you free."

Our Use and Frequent Misinterpretation of Bible Passages and Spiritual Principles

I would like to say something about our use — and often misuse — of Bible passages and spiritual principles. Earlier, I mentioned that there was a time when I repeated passages again and again as if they were affirmations. And they would comfort me and make me feel better, but I didn't understand what I was saying.

I had an experience with the passage, "Thy Grace is my sufficiency in all things." I used to say that passage all day long — over and over again. And my focus was always on "in all things." Then I began to feel self-conscious and somewhat guilty, because I thought I probably shouldn't be implying that I was mainly interested in "in all things." So then, I left off the "in all things," and said, "Thy Grace is my sufficiency." And later, I decided to say simply, "Thy Grace is sufficient." But I still didn't understand what I was saying.

Much later, I placed the passage, "Thy Grace is my sufficiency in all things," in my mind and left it there — without allowing the intellect to continue to try to give me an answer. Leaving all thoughts, ideas, and concerns outside, I gave my attention to the Source Within My Own Being, and became still. Then, when the Spirit "touched" the passage, I realized that Grace isn't something that is poured out upon us or that comes to us as the fulfillment of our designated requirements. It is the pure unconditioned consciousness — The Infinite Invisible Spiritual Energy — flowing through us from the Source as unconditioned form and experience.

You may be familiar with the passage, "Thou wilt keep him in perfect peace whose mind is stayed on Thee." I used to think that meant keeping a Bible passage going in my mind (that is, in my intellect) — regardless of whatever else I was doing. To me, this passage meant "working on two levels" — and just being sure to keep a Bible passage "going" all the time.

I know this doesn't make sense, but I always tried to do whatever I understood something to mean. For a while, I tried my best. But what I was doing certainly was not keeping me in perfect peace.

Apropos of my feeling the necessity of keeping a Bible passage going all the time, there is a story that was told by Charles Fillmore, the founder of the Unity School of Christianity. A man was in a car accident, and as the car was turning over and over, he couldn't think of a Bible passage to say. All he could think of was, "God helps the working girl!" In a crisis, we are apt to pray any kind of "frantic prayer." We think we just have to say "something."

Of course, the intellect has no connection with the Spirit. So, when we are repeating passages again and again in this way, we are just mumbling words that don't mean a thing to us, and don't get us anywhere at all. But after our experience with the Garden of Eden, we've realized the difference between thinking on the surface with the intellect and "centering the mind" on The Infinite Invisible Source — at the Center of Our Very Own Being.

It is obvious that my earlier interpretation of the passage, "Thou wilt keep him in perfect peace whose mind is stayed on Thee," was based on my ignorance and misinterpretation of the meaning of the passage.

Now we have discovered that there must always be an area in our consciousness where the mind is "stayed" on Thee (the Source). You know that this is not the intellect that we are talking about, because the intellect deals only with the outer — with that which has already been formed. It does not deal with the Spirit. But while the intellect is dealing with our daily activities, there is an area in our consciousness where we have an inner awareness of God (the Source), where the mind is "stayed" on Thee.

Joel often spoke of Guru Nanak, who was the founder of Sikhism. There is a poem by a pre-Nanak guru that illustrates the real meaning of the passage, "Thou wilt keep him in perfect peace, whose mind is stayed on Thee." Here is the poem:

A boy gets paper, makes a kite,
And flies it high in the air.
And though he is still talking
In a lively way with his playmates,
His mind is on the string.

Young girls get pitchers
And fill them at the city well,
And they laugh and talk as they carry them.
But their minds are on the pitchers.

The cows stray out of the many gates
Of the city
And graze five miles away from their barns,
But their minds are on their calves.

While the child is asleep in its cradle,
Inside and outside the house
The mother is very busy,
But her mind is on the child.

Do you see that the poem is a perfect example of what the intellect is doing while the mind is stayed on The Source? The intellect is dealing with the outer while the mind is centered on the Infinite Invisible Source Within.

We spoke earlier about placing a Bible passage or a spiritual principle in the mind and leaving it there. We said that when we turn within and become still, the Spirit can then ignite the passage or the principle. When that happens, it has a special significance or message for us. And suddenly, we know the Truth.

You know about the experience I had with the passage, "It profiteth you nothing to pray for your friends, pray for your enemies, if ye would be the children of God." That one passage opened this entire work on love and forgiveness for me. And out of that one passage has come all the tributaries of other passages that have provided corroboration and clarification.

Some passages that corroborate and clarify this work are:

"Forgive seventy times seven."

"Love the Lord Thy God with all thy heart,

with all thy soul, and with all thy mind, and
love thy neighbor as thyself."

"Father forgive them, they know not what they do."

"Forgive us our debts as we forgive our debtors."

"Have that mind in you which was also in Christ
Jesus."

"Resist not evil."

"Put up thy sword."

"Let the one among you who is without sin
cast the first stone."

"If you say you love God, whom you have not seen,
but hateth your brother, whom you have seen,
you are a liar, and the truth is not in you."

"Why beholdest thou the mote that is in thy
brother's eye, but perceiveth not the beam that
is in thine own eye?"

"If you come to the altar to pray and remember
that you have aught against any man, or if
any man has aught against you, rise, make peace
with your brother, and then return to the altar."

Now choose one of the preceding passages and place
it in the mind and leave it there, and let the Spirit

reveal its true meaning. Then let the passage repeat itself to you throughout the day.

There are many more passages that you probably can think of that relate to this work. And there are many, many other passages that you will find helpful to incorporate into your vocabulary. For example:

"Fear not, it is I."

"Speak Lord, Thy servant heareth."

"He that is within me is greater than he that is within the world."

"He performeth that which is given me to do."

"Except the Lord build the house, they labor in vain that build it."

"Awake thou that sleepest, and Christ will give thee light."

You will find it helpful to make a list of as many Bible passages as you can think of, and then add to the list from time to time. If you are not familiar with Bible passages, perhaps you know some passages from other spiritual writings.

We've been speaking about spiritual principles as well as Bible passages, but we haven't explained what we mean by "spiritual principles." All spiritual teachings have principles that are unique to the particular work. For example, two principles that are unique to the teachings of The Infinite Way are: "God constitutes individual Being," and "My conscious oneness with God constitutes my oneness with all Spiritual Being and Idea." There are many other principles in The Infinite Way teaching, but you may place these two principles in your mind — one at a time — and sit in the Silence while you invite the Spirit to confirm the message.

Meditation

I want to suggest a way to use a Bible passage to begin a meditation. With your eyes closed, become still, and let a Bible passage well up from within you. You may simply think of, or choose, a passage, but you will find that there is a difference between thinking of, or choosing, a passage, and letting one present itself as it wells up from within you. Instead of a Bible passage, a spiritual principle may present itself. There's no mystery to this. Just read the following and then experiment with the idea:

> With your eyes closed, turn within and rest here in "the Now."

> Without thinking, let a Bible passage, or a spiritual principle, well up from within you. If no passage presents itself, just think of one.

> Gently ponder the passage — but not for long.

Let the passage or principle rest in your mind, and be still and listen — not for words — but as if you were listening to "feel" a rhythm.

A related or additional passage may or may not come.

You may or may not receive some light or clarification concerning the passage.

Or, you may not feel or be aware of anything at all.

But don't try to make something happen.

Just relax, and without thinking, be still for a few more seconds.

If you wish, you may meditate for a longer period, but don't meditate too long — not more than twenty or thirty seconds. Always end a meditation with Total Stillness — and Complete Silence.

You do not need to feel that you should receive some additional passage or message, or some light or clarification. But you may find that you will spontaneously take a deep breath, or you may simply feel a sense of peace. Or, in the midst of your daily activities, when you least expect it, some idea or "light" may come like a flash "out of the blue."

Glance at the suggestions, and then experiment with the idea again.

Perhaps you have your own approach to meditation. And perhaps you were already meditating every day before you began to read this book. But if you meditate in the morning, have you ever found that when you finish your meditation, you are apt to go through the rest of the day without even thinking of meditating again?

I sometimes say that it is as if we sit under a lamp with the light turned on while we are meditating. And then, when we get up to go about our daily activities, we pull out the plug, and remain in the dark the rest of the day.

Meditating or Pretending to Meditate

When we say, "Let's meditate," have you ever caught yourself closing your eyes and preparing to meditate, but finding that you just can't "get it together"? And so you continue to sit there, pretending to meditate, while you are thinking about all sorts of other things.

We have already quoted a poem by one of the pre-Nanak gurus. There is another poem by a pre-Nanak guru that has meant a great deal to me, and I think you will find it helpful too. It is a vivid example of the experience I've just described. Here is the poem:

> *The snake sloughs its old skin,*
> *But never gets rid of its poison.*
> *Thou, since thy heart is not pure,*
> *Why seemeth thou to meditate,*
> *Repeating the Holy Name?*

> *The crane, standing on one leg,*
> *Still, in the water,*
> *Seemeth likewise to meditate.*
> *She watcheth for fish!*

When we think we are meditating, this poem is a wonderful reminder to check ourselves on whether we may be just "watching for fish." Of course, before we meditate or pray, we should always first remember to ask ourselves, "Am I holding someone in condemnation, or am I refusing to forgive someone?" It isn't very difficult to find a candidate. There probably are many from whom we could choose. But we should select one and "make peace" in our heart before we proceed.

Mini-Meditations

Short, but frequent, meditations are a way of "Keeping the mind stayed on Thee." There are very brief meditations that I use many times each day. I call them my "mini-meditations." They are a way for me to be sure that I don't wander too far off the track, and to enable me to be aware that I am "consciously connected." At the same time, they are my acknowledgment of my oneness with The Infinite Invisible Source Within My Own Being.

Frequently, when I blink my eyes, I consciously let my eyes remain closed an instant or two longer, and I either let a Bible passage or a spiritual principle present itself, or I let well up from within me these words, "I (meaning the personal sense of I) yield to the Spirit," or "Thy Will be done," or "the 'I' at the Center of My Being is one with the Source," or "Now," or "I," or "Is." You may wish to use this idea for "mini-meditations" of your own.

Experiencing "the Now"

Now is not a word. It is an experience. Experiencing "the Now" is one of my most treasured spiritual practices. "The Now" is a perpendicular split-second experience. I step into "the Now" and I abide in the uprightness of the moment. I remain alert, and when thoughts, concerns, and emotions of the horizontal past (whether immediate or remote) try to intrude from behind me, or when thoughts, concerns, or emotions of the horizontal future try to intrude from out ahead of me, I instantly bring my attention back into the perpendicular experience of "the Now" — where I am abiding.

The only contact or experience with God that is possible is in "the Now." God is not in the past. God is not in the future. God is only in "the Now." The past and the future are merely thoughts and emotions. Thoughts, concerns, and emotions of the past or the future may attempt to distract me and usurp the place of the Spirit. But, as I continue to abide in "the Now," I am undisturbed, secure, and serene. Throughout the day, briefly, or for longer periods, I step into "the Now" and I abide there. And if thoughts or emotions of the past or the future intrude, I gently return my attention to the uprightness of "the Now."

Giving Our Attention to God

A great spiritual teacher, with whom I studied very briefly, said something so profound that I have always remembered it. He said, "The only thing we can give to God is our attention."

I looked up the word "attention" and I found that the original meaning is "to stretch the mind toward." This was an illuminating discovery for me.

But where is our attention when we think of God or say the word, "God"? Is it out there someplace? Where is it? This is very important to think about. Our attention should be on The Infinite Invisible Source — at the Center of Our Very Own Being.

What Is Prayer and How to Pray

One of the students asked a question about how to pray. First of all, we will speak about what prayer is not. Prayer is not asking God to do something for us or telling God what we need. God is Omnipresence, Omnipotence,

Omniscience, and therefore, instruction, enlightenment, or advice from us is ludicrous, to say the least.

We have been told, "If you come to the altar to pray, and you remember that you have aught against any man or if any man has aught against you, rise, make peace with your brother, and then return to the altar." This passage tells us exactly what we must do before we can even consider praying. So have I done what I've been told to do? Have I consciously chosen an individual whom I have aught against, or who I feel has aught against me?

And, before I begin to pray, have I gone through the steps of the Procedure for Forgiveness — withdrawing my condemnation, and releasing the individual into his or her Christhood or True Identity? You may think that this has nothing to do with prayer, but it is clearing the way for the Spirit to come forth. And that is really what prayer is.

Prayer is not speaking to God, and asking Him or telling Him what to do. But prayer is removing the blocks that prevent us from receiving the message He has for us. Then we can acknowledge our oneness with God (the Source), and become so still that we can say, "I will listen for Thy Voice." We probably will not actually hear a voice, but we may feel the Presence, or we may have a conscious "experience of oneness," or we may have a sense of peace, or we may find ourselves sponta-neously taking a deep breath. We then sit in the Silence for a few more seconds. And we know we have prayed.

You may feel that you can't accept this kind of prayer. Perhaps you have your own way of praying, and you may not wish to change. You may even say, "I'm not sure that there is a God." Or you may talk to God, and say, "After all this time, and all the study, dedication, and devotion to You, You've deserted me. Or maybe You weren't there in the first place."

There have been times when I've knelt down beside my bed, and prayed out loud, begging, and pleading for an answer — or a solution to a problem. And I know that there may still be other times as well. I'm telling you this, so that if you have your own way of praying, you will feel comfortable as you pray in any manner that seems suitable, appropriate, or satisfactory for you at any given moment.

When You Can't Find the Answer, *Try Looking Within:* *Contemplative Writing*

Do you ever find that you have a problem that you simply can't deal with? You can't meditate, you can't pray, you can't read — you've done everything you know to do, and the situation simply refuses to yield. If you've had such an experience, you may find it helpful — as I have — to sit down and start writing. I sit down with some paper and a pencil and I begin to write exactly what I am experiencing. I may write, "I feel terrible, I feel devastated, and hopeless. I don't know what to do or think. I just want to give the whole thing up. None of this works! I just can't try anymore."

I write whatever I am feeling or thinking — with no reservations. And I don't stop to analyze or ponder or try to write something "spiritual" or what I think I ought to write. I just want an answer — I want a solution to the problem. But as I continue to write, I become aware of "something" within that is on a different level — something that seems to begin to "talk" to me. It's not a voice, but what I'm writing is obviously coming from a different dimension than where I started. And I may find myself writing, "Who is talking?" Then I may write, "That's a weird question! I am asking the question and I want to know the answer." But I don't stop writing. I write absolutely everything that comes through.

Then I may write, "But who is this I who is having the problem? Who is this I who wants to know the answer? And where is this I expecting to find the answer?" Then I may discover that I am writing, "It's the personal sense of I — cut off from the Source — that is talking. It's the personal sense of I that is having the problem. It's the personal sense of I that is expecting the answer to come from the outside."

As I continue to write, I may find that I am writing, "Be still. Look Within." And then I may write, "How can I be still, when I am frantic and scared?" I may want to stop right there, or I may want to continue to argue, saying, "Assure me. I want a sign. I want results."

But I continue to write. Then I may discover that I am writing, "Be still, and know that 'I' — the 'I' at the Center of Your Being — am God. 'I' in the midst of you am mighty. Fear not. It is 'I.' Be at peace. Is there a problem here? 'I' have never left you. 'I' will never leave you nor forsake you. 'I' will be with you until the end of the world."

You will find that writing in this way will be such a vital experience that you will wish to regularly include it as a part of your spiritual practice.

Now, experiment with the idea:

As you sit with some paper and a pen or a pencil, think of something that is bothering you. Begin to write exactly what you are thinking or feeling — regardless of what it is, but don't stop writing. Don't be afraid to write absolutely anything that's going on within you. It's not a matter of trying to pour out all the negativity you can think up. And neither is it a matter of trying to write something spiritual. It has to do with this moment. What is it that is going on in you at this moment? What is it that you can't seem to release?

When you have written for a while, continue to write, but allow "something" within you to begin to "speak." You will recall that I said earlier that it is not an actual voice that you "hear." But it is a kind of message that seems to come from another level within you. Don't sit there and wait for an answer, or a voice or a message. Write the words that come. Just keep on writing. Don't stop, or wait, or think.

Suddenly, it's as if "something" from another place within you begins to come through. Don't stop writing to think or ponder — keep on writing. You can ask questions or "talk back" to this "something." But just keep on writing whatever you find yourself saying or whatever continues to come to you.

Did you find that something like a Presence from Within seemed to acknowledge you and to converse or commune with you? Perhaps you felt that you actually received a message from Within Your Own Being. If you cultivate this practice, you will find that it can take you on into contemplative meditation, which will end in Silence. The purpose of contemplative meditation is to bring us to a point of Stillness so that the Spirit of God Within can take over. You may wish to review the section called "A Contemplative Meditation," which appears earlier in the book.

"Truth Is Within Ourselves"

Here is a quotation from "Paracelsus," by the poet, Robert Browning, which says it all:

> *Truth is within ourselves; it takes no rise*
> *From outward things, whate'er you may believe.*
> *. . . and, to know,*
> *Rather consists in opening out a way*
> *Whence the imprisoned splendor may escape,*
> *Than in effecting entry for a light*
> *Supposed to be without.*

This quotation from Browning will illustrate forever the difference in the way we have been living and the way we are ready to live now. This is "a new way to live."

Whether to Take Human Footsteps or Expect God to Do It

This doesn't mean, however, that we never take human footsteps, and that we simply sit and demand that our designated needs be met "spiritually."

Too often we are apt to get severely out of balance. We prefer the altogether "spiritual route" because, for one thing, it relieves us of the responsibility. And it makes us feel so "spiritual."

There is never a time when we shouldn't do what we know to do. This requires something of us. We are told, "Ye do it." You will find that when you read back over what Jesus told the disciples and the multitudes, it always had to do with "doing something." It involved an activity. As an example, you know that He said, "Pray for your enemies, if ye would be the children of God." Do something yourself. And the Prophet in the Old Testament said to the widow, "Pour the drop that you have." Just always remember this: "Do whatever is at hand to do." If it is one tiny little drop that you have, pour it. And you will find that it primes the pump and gets "the flow" started. But what we usually do is sit there and "blow ourselves up like toads," waiting for God to do it for us.

Doing What Is at Hand to Do

I am going to tell you about an experience that I had years ago at Unity Village, which is located near Kansas City, Missouri. It was, and is, the headquarters of the Unity School of Christianity — founded by Charles and Myrtle Fillmore. I had gone there when I was quite young, without having known anybody who knew anybody who had ever been there. But I went, at the risk of being "disowned" by my parents, who were so upset about it that they wouldn't even tell anybody where I had gone. (We were Methodists in a small Texas town. And even though my parents didn't know anything about Unity, they just disapproved of my going there.)

While I was at Unity Village, I was waiting for the Lord to speak to me concerning what important thing I should be doing. I was sure it was going to be grand and glorious, and I had to be still and sit there and listen.

People at the Village knew I played the piano. I had played at the hotel and at other places too, and they liked to hear me play. And so they began to urge me to give a concert. But of course I wouldn't think of giving a concert because I didn't have time to practice. I had to sit and listen for the Lord to speak. I had to have my attention totally focused, because if the Lord spoke, I might be off playing the piano someplace and not hear the message. So I refused to give a concert, and I got myself in the worst fix imaginable. It was really dreadful.

I had never been so miserable in my life. I wouldn't do anything — because I was just paralyzed, waiting for the Lord to speak. Things were getting worse and worse, and the Lord wasn't speaking at all.

Finally, one day it occurred to me to do what there was at hand to do. Everybody was begging me to give a concert. At least I could do that. So I agreed to give the concert, and I took my music and went down to the recreation hall to practice.

I had played one piece when a young man came in and said, "Do you mind if I listen to you?" I said I didn't mind, and so he sat and listened while I played another piece. And then he said, "Oh, I've always wanted to play the piano. I'd give anything if I could play."

I said, "Come over here, and I'll give you a lesson." We opened the piano bench and got out a Unity songbook, and we sat there together while I gave him a piano lesson. He said, "This is the most marvelous thing I've ever heard of. Does anybody else teach like this?" I said, "No, this is an idea that's come to me, and I have to write a book about it sometime."

Then I said, "And another thing, too, I have an idea for a Keyboard Concealer, so that the students won't watch the keys when they play — somewhat the same principle that is used in teaching typing. But I never have been able to get anything done about it, because I just don't know how to do it." And he said, "I had manual training when I was in school, and I'll help you. You just tell me what you want done."

We hit upon the idea of sticking a piece of paper down between the keys to find out the depth where brackets could rest to hold up a shield. We stuck a piece of paper between the keys on that piano, and then we went to all the pianos around the grounds, testing the depth below the keys. We found that the depth was the same on all the pianos, and that a cardboard bracket would fit between the keys. Of course, a shield could then be supported by a bracket at each end. We got some cardboard and cut something out and worked with this "gadget" we'd made. And in a few days we had something going. We had ourselves a Keyboard Concealer!

I went into town (Kansas City) and spoke to a patent lawyer, and applied for a patent. The lawyer had a search made at the patent office to see if there were anything comparable, and there wasn't. And so, on the Keyboard Concealer, I was allowed seven claims (meaning seven uniquely distinct features), which I was told was quite exceptional.

I never gave the concert I had started out to give. I never had time to give it. But the very fact that I had "finally" done what there was at hand to do opened up this whole experience. I could have been sitting there yet, waiting for the Lord to speak!

Later, I told Joel the story. I said, "I was expecting the Lord to speak, and I wouldn't do anything but sit and wait." And Joel said, "Well, He spoke, all right."

l said earlier that I tell all these stories because I feel that sometimes we remember a story better than we remember a principle itself. I always remember this story as illustrating: "Doing what there is at hand to do."

The Evolution of the Interval Keyblocks

You already know about my inventing the Keyboard Concealer. Several years later, I invented some devices, which I called Interval Keyblocks.

In the town where I taught in Texas, there was a USO. An air base was near the town, and the men who were stationed there spent a lot of time at the USO. I often helped plan the entertainment. The men liked to hear me play the piano, and many of them said, "I've always wanted to play. Won't you teach me?" But, of course there was no time to teach each one who wanted to learn.

As you know, I invented the Keyboard Concealer to keep the students from looking at the keys when they played. I realized, however, that I would have to devise some means for them to coordinate what their eyes were seeing on the music with what their hands (fingers) were "feeling" on the keyboard. And I knew that the solution would have to be based on intervals. An interval is the distance between two notes on the written music, and the distance between two keys on the keyboard.

Every interval is given a number-name. And on the keyboard, you can determine the number-name of the interval by the number of white keys involved. There are 2nds, 3rds, 4ths, 5ths, 6ths, 7ths, and 8ths (or octaves).

For any interval, you always play two keys. It is the distance "between" the two keys that you play that determines the measurement or "feel" of a particular interval. If you subtract the two keys that you play from the number-name of the interval, you will get the number of keys "between."

Each white key is about one inch wide. To play the interval of a 5th, for example, you would subtract the two keys that you play from a 5th (the number-name of the interval), and you will get three keys (about three inches) "between." Set your thumb and your little finger about three inches apart, and notice that your fingers are set to play the two keys of a 5th, leaving three keys (about three inches) "between."

For a 3rd, there is one key (about one inch) "between" the two keys that you play, and you could play the two keys of the 3rd with your thumb and your middle finger. For a 4th, there are two keys (about two inches) "between" the two keys that you play, and you could play the two keys of the 4th with your thumb and your middle finger. Of course, for a 5th, there are three keys (about three inches) "between"; for a 6th there are four keys (about four inches) "between"; for a 7th, there are five keys (about five inches) "between"; and for an 8th, there are six keys (about six inches) "between." You could use your thumb and your little finger to play a 5th, a 6th, a 7th, and an 8th. For the interval of a 2nd, there is no key "between." The two keys of a 2nd are played side by side with two consecutive fingers.

Using the idea for teaching the measurement (or establishing the "feel") of each interval, I was able to teach a lot of the men at one time.

I had a carpenter cut some blocks of wood the size of a white key on the piano. Each block was about one inch wide. I seated the men around ping-pong tables and gave each of them a set of six blocks. They would feel the width of one block for the interval of a 3rd, (pretending to play a key on each side of the block). They would slide two blocks together for the width of a 4th, pretending to play a key on each side of the total width of the two blocks.

In the same way, they would slide the proper number of blocks together for a 5th, a 6th, a 7th, or an 8th and pretend to play the two keys of the interval (one on each side of the total width of the blocks). When they had thoroughly established the "feel" of each of the intervals, they no longer needed to use the blocks. The men loved establishing the "feel" of each of the intervals. And often, when they entered the USO, they would greet me by throwing the measurement of an interval into the air and "freezing their fingers," and having me guess which interval they had formed.

The USO was a Salvation Army Operation. That is, the Salvation Army was responsible for the provision of the supplies and the upkeep and maintenance of the building. Among the available supplies were lots of Salvation Army songbooks. I gave a songbook to each of the men, who were seated at ping-pong tables, and I taught them how to identify the intervals on the music. They had already established the "feel" of each of the intervals, and so, when they saw an interval on the music, their fingers would automatically form the particular interval.

The men practiced on the ping-pong tables, and on their foot lockers in their barracks, and on the desks at the USO — borrowing the songbooks, so they could coordinate the "feel" of the intervals with the way they looked on the music. They were amazed and delighted at what they had learned.

I knew that if I ever wrote and published a book, I couldn't have the wooden blocks as a part of the package. I thought about it a lot. How could I give those who might purchase the book the "feel" of the intervals? I hadn't written the book yet, but I always kept wondering about what I would do.

Sometime later, on one of my trips to New York, I stayed at a hotel where they provided a continental breakfast. Each morning, a box containing a thermos of coffee, a roll, a little jar of jam and a little jar of cream was poked through an opening covered by a hinged metal flap — near the bottom of the door. The jam and the cream were anchored in a small box with two holes cut out on the top of it.

One morning, I looked at the little box that held the jam and the cream, and suddenly, I thought, "That's a 5th!" The little box was exactly the width of three white keys (about three inches). I removed the box and found that it was folded and held together with a tab on each side. I was overjoyed — because I realized that if I ever wrote and published a book, instead of using the wooden blocks, I could use this idea for those who were studying the book to make a little cardboard box for each of the intervals.

The piece of cardboard for each interval could be folded to form a box, and secured with a tab on each side. The box for the 3rd would be the width of one white key; the box for the 4th would be the width of two white keys, and so on for each of the intervals. I called these cardboard boxes or blocks "Interval Keyblocks."

The Evolution of the Interval Keyblocks is really the story of how a necessity led to a series of observations and solutions, which resulted in an exciting discovery.

Much later, I wrote and published *The McClintock Piano Course: A New Experience in Learning*, which includes the Interval Keyblocks and the Keyboard Concealer.

Other Things I Wanted to Do

Although there were lots of other things I wanted to do, physical activities appealed to me the least. Even as a child, I always preferred to sew or paint. And when I went to college, my assortment of excuses for avoiding gym classes was limitless.

A few months before I went to Unity Village, however, much to my surprise, I suddenly became interested in golf. I would go to the golf course early in the morning while the dew was still on the grass and play until the sun was too hot to stay longer. Later in the day, when it was cooler, I'd play again until it was almost dark. When I went to Unity Village, I played golf a lot. One day I played with the women's champion of Missouri, and I beat her!

There's nothing more to say about golf, because when I went home to Texas, someone stole my golf clubs, and I never played again.

Many of the things I did turned out to be brief experiences, but they served their purpose on my journey. And as each experience ended, I immediately moved on to the next — with anticipation.

One day, I got a ride into town (Kansas City). And on the way, I thought, "I've always wanted to design hats, so I'll just see about that now." I was wearing a little $2.98 hat I'd bought on sale — which certainly was no indication that I had any ideas for designing hats at all. But I proceeded to the best department store in Kansas City, and I went directly to the millinery department, and asked to see the buyer. A nice man came out — and I told him that I wanted to design hats. He was extremely kind and patient, and said he didn't know what I could do, but that he'd make arrangements for me to go to a hat manufacturer and ask them to let me use some of their materials to make up some samples for him to see.

He made an appointment for me, and I returned a week or so later and went to the designated place. It was full of lots of people sitting at tables with hat blocks and machines, and whatever else was required as the necessary equipment for making a hat. I was allowed to choose anything I wanted to use to create some hat designs, so I went from shelf to shelf, selecting whatever appealed to me.

I chose a teal blue felt blimp (I called it) — it didn't have a brim — and it was deep enough for me to turn it up so that it was sort of the shape of a Cossack's hat. And I chose a skein of cerise colored wool yarn, which I attached at the top of the hat, and I pulled the skein of yarn down the side and under my chin to the opposite side — so that the yarn could hook into a loop I'd devised of wire and covered with some of the felt.

I didn't know a thing about blocking a hat or any of the professional things you are supposed to know. So, I just sat at a table, in front of a mirror, and put the felt body of the hat on my head and moved it around — twisting and turning it — until I liked the way it looked, and then I pinned it in place.

Another hat that I made was of a soft dark brown felt, which I draped with pale blue silk jersey, letting the fabric hang down the back a little bit. I made another hat of mustard colored beaver felt with a brim, which was far too big, but I folded it in an unusual way, and trimmed it with a skein of a beautiful shade of green wool yarn. I "put together" several hats, and I was pleased with them.

But the people who were working there had been staring at me, and whispering among themselves, obviously wondering who I was, and what on earth I was doing there. I was feeling more and more uncomfortable and disturbed, and suddenly, I became so exhausted that I simply couldn't stay another minute. So I walked out — leaving the hats I had designed on the table where I'd been sitting.

I went back to Unity Village, and about a week later I got another ride into town. I went immediately to the store where I had gone earlier to see about designing hats. When I looked in their window, I saw my hat designs on the mannequins as a part of their display! I couldn't believe it. Of course, I went in and spoke to "my friend." He had no idea that they were my designs. The place where he had sent me had used my designs, and manufactured the hats, and then sold them to him. He was shocked and embarrassed beyond measure at what had happened.

He was impressed, however, with my designs, and he said that there was no doubt that I could be a great hat designer. But he made it clear that I would have to learn the basics of making a hat. He said, "I will be glad to send you to New York and pay for your training. And you can come back and work here, or do whatever you like. But is this what you want to do more than anything else?" I said that I really wanted to teach music in a studio down the street, and that I thought I could design hats "on the side."

He said, "You must think this over, and decide what you want to do more than anything else in the world." I couldn't make my decision on that basis, because I wanted to do it all! I not only wanted to design hats but clothing as well. I wanted to paint and I wanted to teach music. I knew that there were many well-known designers, and that my designs wouldn't be of any special benefit to the world. And of course I knew that there were many really great painters.

So I asked myself what I could do that no one else could do — something that would be of the greatest benefit to the world. I knew that I had an idea for teaching piano that was totally unique — unlike anything that anyone else had ever done — and that it could make it possible for everyone to have a music education. Even though it was a frightening thought, I knew that my decision was made. I chose teaching music.

I will always feel a deep sense of gratitude to "my friend," whose name I don't even recall, for his incredible kindness, thoughtfulness, generous spirit, and insight, and for helping me to turn in the direction I obviously was destined to go.

Just Getting Started

Now that the decision about teaching music had been made, I had the Keyboard Concealer to turn my attention to. (I hadn't yet invented the Interval Keyblocks.) I thought that other teachers would be interested in having their students use the Keyboard Concealer, and I'd have to make it available for them to purchase.

I began to think about the fact that there was a woman who had written some music teaching material that indicated that she would respond to the purpose of my Keyboard Concealer. There were several aspects of her work that made me feel that she would understand my "new" ideas for teaching.

I called her up. She lived in a town near St. Louis, and she said for me to come on the train and get off at a particular stop (just before St. Louis). She told me that she would meet me and take me home with her, and we could talk. So, when all the arrangements had been made, I took off!

She met me at the train station, and took me home with her. I showed her the Keyboard Concealer, and she responded as I had hoped she would. Since she had her own approach to teaching, she immediately envisioned me as representing her and giving workshops on her material, and promoting my Keyboard Concealer at the same time.

So she called her publisher in Cincinnati, and he thought it was all a wonderful idea, but he was leaving for Europe the next day — and would be gone a month. I'd have to wait to see him when he came back. She said that I was welcome to stay with her and wait for him to return from Europe. Of course that was very generous of her, but I felt that it was out of the question.

I realized that I wasn't very far from Indiana, where an artist, whom I knew, had a gallery and studio in an Artists' Colony, part of the year. He had painted some portraits of me when I first went to New York. I admired his work a lot, and it was his paintings that I had exhibited in Texas.

I called him, and he was more than glad that I could come to see him. After spending a few more days discussing the music material for the workshops that I might be giving, and preparing for my meeting with the publisher when he returned from Europe, I left for Indiana.

As soon as I arrived, I greeted my friend, the artist, and I got a room across the street from his gallery and studio. I immediately started painting. Being able to absorb the beauty of his work in the gallery and studio inspired me, and I would go out at dawn and at dusk, and during the day, and even at night, to try to capture the atmosphere he was able to bring to his paintings. I also painted a lot of portraits of local people and those who lived in the surrounding hills — anyone who would pose for me.

I really loved to paint, and during the time that I was there, I ended up with quite a large collection of paintings, a lot of which were later purchased. (Incidentally, many of the landscapes and some of the portraits that I painted, now hang on the walls of my New York apartment.)

I've thought a lot about my painting in Indiana, and I can see that if my attention had been on making money, personal sense might have become so involved that I would not have been able to allow the pure inspiration to come from the Source Within My Own Being.

"An experience of oneness" was the secret. But it is important to remember that the secret of the experience of oneness was brought about by the love and joy of the activity of painting, itself.

The month was up, and the publisher had returned from Europe. He called me, and in a few days, I left Indiana and went to meet him and another man in Cincinnati to discuss plans for my giving the workshops and promoting my Keyboard Concealer. They were very interested in my giving the workshops, but the Keyboard Concealer was a problem that would have to be dealt with by their main office in New York.

So I went to New York. The head of the New York office was a woman, who had her own teaching materials. She used a totally different approach, which did not accommodate my Keyboard Concealer. And she told me that the New York office was not interested in it. Obviously, since I would not be able to promote my Keyboard Concealer, I would not consider their offer to have me give the workshops.

Meanwhile, I'd heard about a company in Chicago that I thought might be interested in the Keyboard Concealer. When I was at Unity Village, a lovely lady from Chicago more or less "adopted" me. I called her from New York, and she was happy at the prospect of my coming to see her. So I went to Chicago. Sure enough, the company was interested in the Keyboard Concealer, and they immediately offered me a contract. At last, I had a manufacturer.

I went back by Unity Village, where they had an exhibition of my paintings, and then home to Texas for the holidays.

You may feel that I have written too many extraneous stories that have nothing to do with "Love and Forgiveness." But each of my adventures and explorations has been an important part of my journey. And each one has provided me with experiences and insights that have expanded my spiritual growth.

The pursuit of a manufacturer for the Keyboard Concealer provided me with the experience of "perseverance." I never gave up!

My Introduction to The Infinite Way

Now I would like to talk about my introduction to The Infinite Way, which I had not yet discovered. When I first read Joel Goldsmith's book, *The Infinite Way*, I was quite excited about it. But then, after I finished reading the book, I remembered that, someplace in it, Joel had said that you couldn't use this for yourself. I liked all the rest of it, but I couldn't see what good it was if you couldn't use it for yourself. So I closed the book and didn't open it again for a long time — because I still wanted to "demonstrate." I wanted to get what I wanted. I wanted to use it for myself, and I didn't understand why I couldn't.

As I recall, I was always "wanting" something. And earlier I had discovered some metaphysical teachings that told me how I could get or "demonstrate" what I wanted. I was delighted, and I followed all the steps with great diligence. I learned and recited lots of affirmations and denials. I was thrilled and enthusiastic, because "it really seemed to work." But after a while "it" didn't work anymore. I couldn't "demonstrate" a thing. I was discouraged and disappointed, and I couldn't understand what had happened.

I began to read some books in which we were told clearly that we shouldn't "desire" anything. Then I was totally confused. How could I not desire or want something? As a matter of fact, it was at this point that I realized that The Infinite Way wasn't for me — because my only interest was to use it for myself and to get what I wanted. I had come far enough, however, to see that we couldn't expect God to answer our prayers and give us what we told Him we wanted. But not having desires was something else. How could this be?

It was much later that I realized that "having desires" was totally connected to living humanly. If we "desire" or "want," we are experiencing separateness — and we are attempting to get something, or to appropriate something to add to ourselves. If we are living spiritually, however, we are aware that we are already complete. And we are fulfilled because we know that we are "experiencing oneness" with God — with All That Is. When I observe that I am "desiring" or "wanting," I must realize that I have forgotten that the "I that I am" (My True Identity) is "at one" with the Source.

Throughout my search, the one prayer that I always prayed was, "Father, don't let me kid myself." Maybe this is kind of a silly prayer, but this is what I always prayed, "Don't let me kid myself. I don't want to think I know something that I don't know. Please don't let me miss anything. Let me know and do whatever there is to be known and done."

Light Begins to Dawn on Some Bible Passages

I always liked the Bible passage that said, "A thousand shall fall at thy left and ten thousand at thy right, but none of these things shall come nigh thy dwelling place." This passage really gave me a sense of security and assurance.

But then I asked myself, "Did this passage say anything specific about whose dwelling place it did not come nigh?" Suddenly, I saw that the passage actually said that it does not come nigh the dwelling place of the one who abides in "the Secret Place of the Most High."

I could now see that unless I am living spiritually — abiding in the Secret Place of the Most High — it is just as apt to come nigh my dwelling place as the dwelling place of anyone else. This realization "shook me up." But at least I knew that there was no choice. I had to live spiritually.

One day I read the Bible passage, "I of myself can do nothing, but the Father within, He doeth the work." I didn't really understand the passage at all, but I knew that it contained a significant message for me. Much later, I realized that when Jesus said, "I of myself can do nothing," He was speaking of the personal sense of I. And when He said, "But the Father within, He doeth the work," He was speaking of the "I that I am" — the Spirit of God Within His Own Being.

By this time, I had realized that my attempt at what I thought was spiritual practice, was simply trying to "demonstrate" (that is, trying to get what I wanted) — which couldn't be considered spiritual practice at all. But there was something within me that was willing to see things in a new way.

I used to think that Grace was when something came to me that I wanted — like getting a seat by a window on the plane or getting a good parking place.

Then I placed the word "Grace" in my mind and became still — without letting the intellect try to give me an answer. And I found that the word had a whole new meaning for me. I felt that Grace is when Love, Forgiveness, Givingness, and the Consciousness of Oneness are flowing through me and out to the world. So that Grace is not getting a good parking place, but it is forgiving the person who took the one I was headed for.

Different Levels of Consciousness

You know that when we first become aware of a Bible passage, or when we first read a book or listen to a recording, we usually are interested only in what will benefit us, and in what appeals to us at the particular time. We really don't pay much attention to anything else. We like to read and listen to all the "good" things that we might be fortunate enough to have happen to us. We go all the way through a book or a recording, and this is all we are aware of. We really don't see or hear anything else at all.

But some time later, we can think of the same principle or Bible passage, read the same book, or listen to the same recording, and all of a sudden say, "How on earth did that get there? I've repeated that Bible passage, and I've read that book, and listened to that recording dozens of times, and I never saw or heard that before. It's as if it simply hadn't been there!"

The experience may be compared to following a red thread all the way through, just looking for what we want for ourselves. But as our consciousness changes, we are able to "see and hear things" from another level. And then, we no longer follow the red thread, but it's as if we have begun to follow a yellow thread. We may not realize it, but when we were following the red thread, we were functioning on one level of consciousness, and now that we are following a yellow thread, we are functioning on a totally different level. Then, as our consciousness continues to change, we may follow a silver thread, or even a gold thread. And with each change of consciousness, we are able to discern more advanced levels of Truth.

An illustration that I often use concerns the railroad tracks. If you lie down and look down the railroad tracks, they appear to come together very quickly. But if you stand up, you can see that they don't come together quite as quickly as you thought they did. And then, when you rise even higher, onto a totally different level, you see that the tracks don't come together at all. But then you don't need the tracks anyway. You are using a whole new form of transportation.

My Response When I Took Another Look at The Infinite Way

Later I read the book, *The Infinite Way*, again. Meanwhile, my consciousness had changed, and I understood why Joel had said we couldn't use it for ourselves. I understood why I couldn't use it to get what I wanted. In the first place, it won't work, because we cannot use God. And in the second place, if we've been expecting God to enter the human scene to answer our requests — there is no such God.

What am I looking for? Doesn't it seem obvious? Doesn't it seem ridiculous that I've been knocking myself out trying to get something to come to me from the outside?

The Kingdom of Heaven is already within us. The Infinite Invisible Spiritual Energy, the Rhythm, the Life Current, the Givingness, the Forgivingness, and the Love are within us. This is an Invisible Substance, and as It flows forth through us, It forms whatever the need for the moment happens to be.

We don't really know what we need. But the Spirit within us knows. Joel said, "How in the world could Moses have thought up praying for a cloud by day and a pillar of fire by night?" He couldn't have thought it up, he couldn't have dreamed it up, he couldn't have prayed for it. So the answers are presented to us according to the need.

The Solution for Meeting Any Situation

Students often say to me, "I don't know how to meet this particular situation. What would you do?" And my answer always is, "I do what I know to do."

And of course, the first thing that I know to do is to ask myself if there is someone I am still holding in bondage — someone I haven't forgiven — or someone with whom I haven't "made peace in my heart." If we want the Spirit to come through, it is we who have to clear the way. I may not know all the steps, but if I've done what I know to do, I can be assured that the rhythm has begun. And the rhythm then takes over and carries me forward.

Many times, instead of preparing the way for the Spirit to take over, we pitch right in and try to "think it all through" ourselves. Then the intellect is in charge — and we become a function of the intellect and the senses.

We always need to remember that the intellect and the senses were given to us to deal with the outer. And so if I'm going to "think it through" and live by the intellect, the best I can ever hope for is something that has already been formed. I may get different combinations, but there is nothing fresh — there is nothing new. If I "think it up," it will never be from the Spirit. It's already stale. It's already used up.

So, instead of thinking — putting one thought up against another thought — we must "still" the intellect. We turn away from the outer (that which has already been formed), and we give our attention to the Source at the Center of Our Being — Omnipresence, Omnipotence, Omniscience. And as we rest there, we allow the answer to flow forth pure, fresh, and unconditioned.

A Reminder About Forgiveness, Non-Condemnation, and Non-Judgment

It's been quite a while since we've mentioned forgiveness, non-judgment, and non-condemnation. But we have to constantly remind ourselves that if we are still refusing to forgive, and if we are continuing to indulge in judgment and condemnation, we are cutting ourselves off from the Source. We are "As a branch that is cut off and withereth." We can close our eyes and say, "Omnipresence, Omnipotence, Omniscience" till doomsday, and we will just be saying words.

When we see how easy it is for us to forget and to return to our old habits, we can understand that those whom we are judging and condemning can't keep from doing what they are doing. How can we judge or condemn, or refuse to forgive? We are all subject to the same universal mesmerism.

Are you continuing to add to your lists? We never get through, you know. But it's not just a matter of adding to the lists. We have a habit of saying we will "put them on the list." And then what do we do about it? We have to go through the steps of the Procedure for Forgiveness with every one on the lists. You may say, "That will take me from now on." Well, what else is there to do?

I know that I have so much to be forgiven for, and I know too that I can be forgiven only as I forgive others. Sometimes, when I look at the names on my lists, I think of each individual as offering me a gift. Each one is giving me an opportunity to forgive them. And by my forgiving them, I, myself, am forgiven.

Have you ever discovered that even though you know and understand exactly what to do, you are often tempted to disregard or ignore the very thing you have the most profound intention of doing?

Joel told me once that "We never get beyond temptation." This was a great shock to me. I always thought that sometime I would "arrive," and that I would be blissfully exempt from all the responsibilities and problems of "this world." But I've discovered that there is "no way out." All the exits are blocked.

A Transforming Experience

Soon after I came to New York to live — and before I had found The Infinite Way, and before I had discovered the importance of forgiveness, non-condemnation, and non-judgment — I went on a two-week retreat with a group of "truth seekers."

The event was held on a beautiful estate owned by a wealthy man whose mansion was made available as a residence for some of those who attended the retreat. I was privileged (I thought) to be chosen to stay there. I had an elegant room with a private bath. The activities and all the meetings were held near a dormitory-like facility where others were staying. My problem, however, was that the mansion was not too accessible to that area.

I hadn't realized that drinking and smoking were forbidden. The drinking was no problem for me — I didn't drink anyway. But being forbidden to smoke certainly was a problem.

I was an avid smoker. And for several years, I had tried to give it up on various occasions — once, even for Lent, which I had never observed for any other reason. I really did want to stop smoking, but I was one of those who would go out in a blizzard to buy cigarettes if I had run out. And in a real emergency, I would rummage in my waste baskets for a discarded cigarette stub and smoke it, holding it with a bobby pin.

At the mansion where, of course, smoking was forbidden, I would stuff towels along the bottom of the door to keep the smoke from getting out into the hall. And I would open the bathroom window and stand up and smoke — blowing the smoke out the window.

My constant concern was how to get back and forth from the meetings to the mansion. It was foremost in my mind at the meetings to locate someone who might take me to the mansion so that I could have a cigarette. In my thoughts and emotions, I was blaming and accusing literally everyone at the meeting for what I considered to be their responsibility in depriving me of being able to smoke. I found myself disliking and condemning all of those holier-than-thou truth seekers. And I wished I had never heard of them in the first place.

The one thing that I derived from the meetings, however, was that you had to commit yourself — actually saying, "I give my life to God." You didn't have to stand up and say it at the meeting — or even to anyone else. You simply had to say it. But I just couldn't do it!

A day or two before the retreat was to be over, I determined that I would say it. On the particular morning, I was in the bathroom, and I held onto the towel rack, and I said it out loud, "I give my life to God!" I fully expected the earth to crumble. But nothing happened. I didn't feel a bit different — except the relief that I had actually done it. However, later, I had a transforming experience that I felt was directly related to my ability to finally have the courage to make the commitment "to give my life to God."

I returned home to New York, and sometime later, I was reaching for my package of cigarettes, and all of a sudden I literally stopped in my tracks. A very powerful feeling swept over me — accompanied by these words, "I am being a function of a cigarette." I thought, "I wouldn't let anyone or anything else control me like that!" And I stopped smoking "cold turkey" — and have never smoked since.

As you know, previously, I had unsuccessfully tried every conceivable way to give up smoking — and nothing worked. I certainly didn't say, "I give my life to God" as another way of trying to give up cigarettes. But "something" obviously changed my consciousness — thereby changing my experience. And my problem with smoking was eradicated.

Much later, I lived in an apartment with a woman who was out of town a lot. When she was at home we often had guests for dinner, and she thought we should always have cigarettes available for the guests. She occasionally smoked a cigarette when we didn't have guests, and there usually was a package of cigarettes on the kitchen table.

One day, while she was away on a trip, I was wiping off the table, moving the package of cigarettes around with the salt and pepper shakers and other items. Suddenly, I thought, "For weeks, I've been moving that package of cigarettes around, without even being aware of what it was." It had no more power over me than the salt and pepper shakers!

I've just realized, after writing this, that when I made my list of those I had condemned, I never put those people who were attending the retreat on my list. But now I still can — and I must. I can go through the steps of the Procedure for Forgiveness until I arrive at an "experience of oneness" with each one of them.

I now see how ridiculous it was for me to condemn everyone at the retreat. I made the whole episode absurd. I know that I can't forgive myself. But I can find others (many, as a matter of fact) who I think I just can't forgive — and forgive them. There is no choice. I must establish an "experience of oneness" with each one who attended the retreat. And I will — starting right now.

Observing Whether I Am Reacting or Responding

When a situation arises that irritates us, or hurts our feelings, or seems endless or insurmountable, what do we do? Of course, we usually react.

I have suggested to the students that we ask ourselves, "Am I reacting or am I responding? Do I prefer to keep on rehearsing the situation — going over and over and over it — as I continue to indulge in my reaction? Or, instead of reacting with anger, hurt feelings, resentment, or frustration, do I realize that I can stop it instantly by consciously responding with non-judgment, non-condemnation, and forgiveness?"

You will recall our earlier discussion about living humanly and living spiritually. We said that when we are living humanly, we are acted upon from the outside (the arrows point inward toward the circle). And when we are living spiritually, we are living from the inside outward (the arrows point outward from the circle). We always need to watch which way the flow is going. We should let the Spirit flow outward so forcefully that nothing can swim upstream. When non-judgment, non-condemnation, forgiveness and love flow through us and out from us, we have "dominion." The word dominion comes from *Dominus*, which means God. And God is the Source — at the Center of Our Very Own Being.

We have a choice. Just ask yourself, "Am I reacting, or am I responding?" If I am reacting, I am allowing myself to be "acted upon" from the outside, and I am living humanly. But if I am responding, I am inviting the Spirit to flow forth from within — outward — to bless and to heal. I am then living spiritually, and I have dominion. I can relax and rest in a state of "Is."

Condemning Others to a State of Consciousness

One of the students asked me this question: "Is a negative thought about a person condemning them?" And my answer was that there are two ways of condemning. We condemn individuals *for* something: *for* doing something or *for not* doing something. And another way is condemning them *to* a state of consciousness. For example, we condemn them to an illness, to an attitude, to thoughtlessness, to selfishness, to a kind of disposition, to age, to carelessness, to being nosey, to being "a know-it-all," and on and on and on. We categorize them, and we always think of them in the same way.

We can't even condemn anyone to the limitation of our highest concept of good for them. I've told the story many times about an experience I had with someone I knew who had a great gift — a great talent. And I hadn't realized that I had held them so rigidly to my own concept of what I felt was the highest good for them, that I had succeeded in absolutely paralyzing them. They were afraid to take a step of any kind for fear they wouldn't live up to what I thought they ought to be doing. I was condemning them to a state of consciousness that made them incapable of receiving freedom and inspiration from the Source —Their Own Inner Being. Who in the world did I think I was?

You see, when we condemn others to a state of consciousness, we are "boxing them into" our judgment of them. And anytime we see them or think of them, we are always alert to register whether they are "living up" (or down) to our predictions. Have you ever noticed that we will condemn someone *for* doing something, and then we will condemn them *to* the state of consciousness in which we expect them to continue to do the same thing?

Have you ever said, or thought, "Now just look at that! Isn't that just like them? Wouldn't you know it? That's just what I knew they would do. Didn't I tell you?" We may not realize it, but if we condemn another to a particular state of consciousness, we are condemning ourselves as well. As I do to another, I do to myself.

One of the most subtle habits is "condemning someone for condemning." Have you ever caught yourself saying or thinking, "One thing I simply can't stand is that he (or she) is constantly condemning."? Once, a student, whose co-worker was condemning someone all the time, asked me if she should speak to the co-worker about the habit she had of condemning. My reply was, "Are you condemning her for condemning? And do you see that you are condemning her to a state of consciousness in which she always condemns?" The student was stunned. A Bible passage that would be appropriate here is: "And why beholdest thou the mote that is in thy brother's eye, but perceiveth not the beam that is in thine own eye?"

Often, students say to me that they are having a miserable experience with someone. And they know that I am going to mention the word "forgiveness," so they say immediately, "I have forgiven him (or her) — I really have."

Someone said, "We've been married twenty-five years, and he has *always* been like that." Then I pointed out to the student that she may have forgiven her husband *for* what he is doing (or has done), but that she is still condemning him *to* the state of consciousness that makes him continue to do what he has "always" done.

Now we will make a list of the names of those we have been, or are, condemning *to* a state of consciousness. And beside each name, we will write what we have been, or are, condemning him or her to. We may find that we are condemning them to an illness, to age, failure, selfishness, stubbornness, thoughtlessness, laziness, negativity, addictions, objectionable habits, and on and on. You will think of other qualities, characteristics, or limitations that you wish to add. And from time to time, you will also be able to add other names as you think of them.

For your list, write this heading:

Those I have been, or am, condemning to a state of consciousness.

And now follow through with the procedure suggested in the preceeding paragraph. As you write the name and the state of consciousness to which you have been, or are, condemning each one, ask yourself, "Does this state of consciousness, by any chance, apply to me?"

When you have finished writing the names and the state of consciousness to which you have condemned each one, look at each name again and say, "I withdraw my condemnation and judgment. And with love (an experience of oneness) the 'I that I am' releases you into your Christhood or True Identity. God constitutes your Being."

States of Consciousness to Which I Condemn Myself

Of course, there are lots of kinds of relationships and many situations in which we condemn others to a particular state of consciousness. And we must not forget that we condemn ourselves to limitations, qualities, and characteristics as well. For example, we may condemn ourselves to being lazy, to being a workaholic, to feeling unappreciated, misunderstood, unloved, to being a victim, or unlucky. We may condemn ourselves to being addicted to certain foods, cigarettes, alcohol, or drugs. We may condemn ourselves to being addicted to exercise, shopping, the TV, movies, credit cards, the Internet, or cell phones. And you will think of many others.

Now, make a list, using this heading:

The limitations, qualities, and characteristics to which I condemn myself.

Leave plenty of room to write lots more, because you may not be able to think of many things at first. Making the lists may not immediately release us from our addictions and limitations, but seeing the lists will make us more alert.

Do I realize that the limitations to which I have condemned myself are not of my True Identity? And do I realize that the limitations to which I have condemned others are not of their True Identity? We cannot deny, however, that they are a part of humanhood.

Are you aware that there is nothing we can do about humanhood except to rise up out of it. But the "catch" is, we can't rise up and be released as long as we are holding others in bondage to our judgment of them. Our own judgment, condemnation, and lack of forgiveness "weigh us down."

"Judge Not by Appearances,
Judge Righteous Judgment"

What do we do? The passage, "Judge not by appearances, judge righteous judgment" is the answer. Judge not by appearances means that I do not judge the qualities and limitations of another individual, or of myself.

I do not condemn others to their humanhood (that is, to their sense of separation from God), and neither do I condemn myself to my humanhood (to my sense of separation from God). But I judge righteous judgment.

What is righteous judgment? Righteous judgment means that the "I that I am" recognizes that "God constitutes individual Being." It is important to begin with the principle, "God constitutes individual Being" and then recognize that the principle applies not only to the Being of the specific individual that I have been condemning, but to My Own Being as well.

When I say, "God constitutes individual Being," I must be sure that I am not just saying or thinking words. I must be still enough to let the Spirit reveal to me what and where God is. Omnipresence, Omnipotence, Omniscience constitute and manifest as individual Being right here where I am, and where the individual is that I am, or have been, condemning.

Withdrawing My Condemnation

If I have been condemning another to limitations of any kind, I must ask myself the question, "Does such limitation exist in God — Omnipresence, Omnipotence, Omniscience?" Since God constitutes and manifests as individual Being, the limitation to which I have been condemning the individual cannot exist. It looks as if I've made it all up! This is simply the universal hypnotism, which the personal sense of I has accepted. So I can now say, "I withdraw my condemnation. I no longer condemn you to your humanhood — the sense of separation from God. With love (an experience of oneness) the 'I that I am' releases you into your Christhood — your True Identity."

I am the one who is told not to judge by appearances, but to judge righteous judgment. I am not responsible for what happens to the one from whom I've withdrawn my judgment and condemnation. The individual that the "I that I am" releases into his or her True Identity may or may not change — but I will. My own consciousness will change. You have read this many times: When consciousness changes, the form and experience change.

About Worry

A form of "condemning to a state of consciousness" that is often overlooked derives from "worry." There are countless situations, individuals, and problems of all kinds that can absorb us with worry. As an example, parents usually worry about their children from the time they are born. They worry about their health and safety, and later, when the children are in school, they add the worry about their grades and their relationships. Still later — when the children become teenagers — the ingredients of suspicion and fear may be added, because the parents are beginning to condemn their children to a state of consciousness in which they do not trust them. They worry about what the children are doing or not doing, and they are afraid the children will get into trouble of some kind. Of course, the parents are actually creating a negative atmosphere that is condemning their children to the very situation they wish to avoid.

This does not mean, however, that they should not exercise parental responsibility — including guidance, discipline, and setting boundaries.

Strange as it may seem, the most difficult — but priceless — gift parents have to give is relinquishing worry and recognizing that God constitutes the Being of their child, and the Being of his or her peers.

There Is "No God And" There Is Only "God As"

The following section illustrates two principles of The Infinite Way: "No And," and "As."

One of the students called and said, "I am so worried about my aunt. She is in the hospital, and the doctors can't find out what is the matter with her. Even though I have been studying and meditating for years, I simply don't know what to do. But I know that God is with her."

I asked, "Do you think God is *with* her?" She replied that she did. Then I said, "Are you aware that your words indicate that you think there is God *and* your aunt, and that God — separate and apart from your aunt — is with her?" Statements such as, "I know that God is with her," are comforting, but they are not based on a spiritual principle. Without realizing it, the student was condemning her aunt to a state of consciousness of being separate and apart from God. I repeated the principles, "God constitutes individual Being" and "God manifests as individual Being." Then I asked the student, "Do you now understand that there is no God *and* your aunt? There is only God manifesting *as* your aunt."

I had a reminder of this principle once when I was going to Hawaii to see Joel. I woke up early on the morning of my departure, and I said, out loud, "Father, be with me." And the Voice responded, "How can I be *with* you? I *am* you."

You see, we are simply returning to the awareness of the truth of our Being. We are remembering who and what we are, and who and what everyone else is. We must do this for ourselves so that we can be a transparency through which the Spirit can flow forth to heal and to bless.

Our Responsibility for the Government

What about the government? Do we realize that we all have a responsibility for the government? But are we constantly condemning and judging? If we are, do we realize that we are contributing to exactly what we are condemning? We watch what is happening and we observe whether "they" are doing what we predicted they would do or would not do.

Of course we not only condemn them *for* doing something or *for not* doing something, but we condemn them *to* a state of consciousness that ensures that they will continue to do what they "always" do, or do not do.

Let's make a list of the officials and employees of the government (national, state, city, and community) that we are condemning. Some of the names may have already appeared on our original lists, but we will include them again on this special list.

Now write this heading:

Those in the government (national, state, city, and community) that I have been, or am, condemning or judging.

And now, under the heading, proceed to write as many names as you can think of at this time — leaving room to add others later. Then, using the steps of the Procedure for Forgiveness that were suggested for the other lists, withdraw your condemnation. And finally, acknowledging that God constitutes individual Being, release each one into his or her Christhood or True Identity.

Our Responsibility for Our World Including the Criminals and the Terrorists

What do we do about those whose names are in the news for committing some terrible crime? How do we deal with them? Are we just going to say, "Isn't this terrible! Isn't this the worst thing you ever heard of?" That is a reaction. But what is my response? Judge not! There is the temptation to say, "Well, I can't forgive that. I never did anything that bad." That is not the point. There is no way for us to get out of this now. If we are on this Path, we have to keep going.

So what do I do? I know exactly what to do. I ask myself, "What have I done that I wish I hadn't done?" or "What didn't I do that I wish I had done?" I start right there. And then I ask myself, "Why did I do what I did?" or "Why didn't I do what I wish I had done?"

The same universal mesmerism that functions in me functions in the individual that I am condemning — regardless of what the incident or situation is. The mesmerism may not have manifested in the same way in both of us. But who knows how it may have manifested in me at some other time, or in some previous existence? Who knows what I may need to be forgiven for that is beyond my remembrance? But by forgiving someone else for whatever it is that they have done, or have not done, I can cancel out something for myself.

You may say, "Well, what is going to happen? Shouldn't the criminals and terrorists be punished?" I know that Joel said that such individuals should be kept from doing the same thing again. But that does not prevent me from forgiving them. I must always remember that if I refuse to forgive, I am cutting myself off from the Source.

And so I have to know that this has been the universal mesmerism or hypnotism. This has not been of the True Identity of the one who has committed the terrible crime that we have been talking about. What I have to do now is to realize that "God constitutes individual

Being," and therefore God constitutes the Being of this individual. The same God that constitutes My Being constitutes the Being of the one I've condemned.

You will recall that we said earlier that we are not free to enter back into the Kingdom if we are holding anyone else out. We must not judge by appearances. We must judge righteous judgment. And righteous judgment means that God constitutes individual Being. We can say "God constitutes individual Being" again and again and again. But we have to keep on until we have come to a point of stillness where "something" wells up from within us and says, "Yes, God *does* constitute individual Being, and God constitutes the Being of the one I have been condemning."

The individual I must forgive may be the one I've called a liar or a thief or a criminal or a terrorist. But there is "something" that remembers that we are One. It is the same God, the same Source, that constitutes My Being and their Being, and the Being of everyone on this earth. That Thread, that Center, that Spark, that Core is the same in all of us. That is where we are One.

Everything that we hear about or read about is an opportunity for us not only to free ourselves, but also to lift up the consciousness of mankind. We cannot shut ourselves off from what is happening in the world.

Where there is crime, there are so-called criminals. And the world cannot be free unless the consciousness of criminals and terrorists is changed and lifted up. We must be alert and remember that we have a responsibility, which is: "Judge not by appearances, judge righteous judgment." We must lift up each individual into his or her Christhood.

When the "I that I am" has released the individual into his or her Christhood, I can love my neighbor as myself. Then the Spirit can "light up" the spiritual principle, and I know the Truth, which makes us both free.

Often, students say, "What should I do when I witness or hear about a crime?" First of all, I must realize that regardless of appearances, the individual is being functioned by the same universal mesmerism or hypnotism to which I am subject or vulnerable. And I must realize that the same God that constitutes my Being constitutes the Being of the criminal or the terrorist. Therefore, difficult as it is, I must admit that we are One. Then I consciously withdraw my condemnation, and with love (an experience of oneness), the "I that I am" releases the individual into his or her Christhood or True Identity.

Our acknowledgment and recognition of who they really are can allow those who are receptive to awaken — and their consciousness to be transformed. Since we are all One, the transformation of the consciousness of one individual can contribute toward the transformation of the consciousness of all mankind.

When we speak of the so-called criminals or terrorists, we are apt to think of them as worthless and of no value to the world. There is an analogy that I frequently use. You know what a flower bulb looks like. It is the most unpromising-looking object imaginable. And yet, you know that within the flower bulb are the leaves and the buds and the blossoms and the colors and even the fragrance. But if we don't recognize its true nature and all that is within it, it remains just a flower bulb. And we are apt to toss it out. But when we judge "righteous judgment" — instead of judging by appearances — we will plant the bulb and nourish it, which is actually releasing it into its True Identity (the Spiritual Nature of its Being). And of course, we, ourselves, are blessed and nourished as well.

We may still say, "I can't do it! I can't help it. I just cannot forgive criminals and terrorists." We know that Jesus said, "Father, forgive them, they know not what they do." And we know that when He spoke of the Father, He was referring to the Spirit of God Within His Being. Of course, the personal sense of I can't forgive — but the "I that I am" at the Center of My Being can.

You may be familiar with the passage, "Have that mind in you which was also in Christ Jesus." You know that Jesus said, "Let the one among you who is without sin cast the first stone." And He also said, "Neither do I condemn thee."

Once, I was feeling more deeply affected than usual by the realization that I had "wrongly accused" so many and had locked them into the prison of my judgment and condemnation. Suddenly, I felt as if I were going through the halls of the prison — in my own consciousness — unlocking one cell door after another as I withdrew my judgment and released into his or her Christhood each one I had condemned. And as I freed each "prisoner," I found that I had freed myself.

It seems to me that this work is almost as if an "Order of Purification" is being established on earth. Only your own Inner Being — the Spirit Within — could have prepared and drawn you to this place in consciousness. And since you have read this far in the book, you are to be a part of, and a contributor to, this experience for all mankind.

Making Corrections

You may think that when we do this work, we should never make corrections. But we certainly shouldn't allow ourselves to be milque-toasts or door-mats. There are times when corrections are necessary — and they should not be avoided. Parents have a responsibility to guide and discipline their children, and of course, teachers have a responsibility to correct their students. And we should always feel free to request the highest quality not only of service, but also of the products that we purchase.

The Saga of the Skirt

I often tell about an experience I had that describes how I made a correction. Soon after I came to New York, I went home to Texas for a visit. While I was there, my parents took me to Dallas and bought me a suit at

Neiman Marcus. At that time, the most fashionable skirts were long and very narrow. When I returned to New York, I wore the suit, but I found that the skirt was so narrow that I could hardly get up and down the curb.

One Sunday, I wore the suit, and went with a friend to St. Thomas Church. We knelt down to say our prayers, and I couldn't get up. I had to lean back onto my elbows so that I could pull myself up enough to hoist myself back into the seat.

Later, I wore the suit to a tea party, where I had another embarrassing experience. At the party, I was introduced to the editor of a well-known fashion magazine. I wanted to sit beside her while we talked, but since I was holding my refreshment plate, I was unable to use both hands to slide my skirt up so that I could bend enough to sit down. When I left the party, I went out to get a cab, but I found that I couldn't step up into it. So I had to swing in on the strap — and I sprained my wrist.

This seemed just about "the end" — to have this expensive suit and to be stuck with it in this way. And so I spent half a day composing a letter to Stanley Marcus. I told him that I had always looked forward to owning a suit from Neiman Marcus, and that my parents had bought this suit for me, but that it was actually dangerous to wear it in New York, where one had to be free to run at any moment when crossing the street. I related all the disastrous experiences I'd had, and I mailed the letter.

Before I realized that they'd had time to receive the letter, I had a phone call from the Neiman Marcus New York office, saying that the designer of the suit wanted to pick up the skirt and redesign it. The designer sent for the skirt, and redesigned it, and returned it to me. And the following season, a two-column story appeared in *The New York Times,* saying that this particular well-known designer had found "ways for easy walking in spite of slim shaping."

Perhaps you think that you, as an individual, or that I, as an individual, can't do anything about such a situation. But I feel that we actually have a responsibility. It does take time, however, to write an appropriate letter. But it is worth it. I've often thought about the fact that the letter I wrote had a very important impact on the fashion industry — as well as the comfort and "safety" of the women who later purchased the suits.

"Cool Off" Before You Make a Correction

I never hesitate to make corrections. But when I make a correction or suggestion — whether I am speaking to someone or writing a letter — I must be sure that I have waited until I've "cooled off" so that there is no anger or negativity remaining. If there is anger, I know that personal sense is at work. And the individual who is the recipient of my correction will react and strike back.

The quickest way to "cool off" is to ask ourselves if we have ever done anything that we shouldn't have done, or if we have always done everything we should have done — or if we have always been so perfect. These questions will switch our attention and allow us to calm down.

Of course, we may "enjoy" the excitement and stimulation of the anger we feel when we are "standing up for ourselves" and "telling someone off." But we must realize what we are doing — we are cutting ourselves off from the Source.

Someone called me recently about a situation that we had been working on for some time, and he said, "Now should I write a letter and say that I don't think you should have done that?" And I said, "Don't do it yet, because there is still too much residue of the anger connected with it. And a letter would only stir the situation up again. When you know that you have forgiven them, and that you are dealing strictly with the principle, you will be able to articulate what you have to say without negativity of any kind. Then you can write the letter — if you are still inclined to do so." But lots of times, the hardest thing in the world to do is to keep from "blowing up" immediately about a situation, or to keep from blurting out something that we later regret — but try to justify.

When I wrote the letter about the skirt, I didn't know about the forgiveness work. And even though I had a legitimate complaint, and my letter simply told the story of my experience, I certainly did not think of forgiveness in relation to it. Now, of course, I do know about the forgiveness work. And so, before I write a letter, or make a correction, I know that I must realize that condemnation is involved, and that I must not proceed until I have followed through with the steps of the Procedure for Forgiveness. Then I can be sure that it is not "personal sense" that is writing the letter, or making the correction. And I will be able to see and articulate the principle more clearly.

I know that there is a lot of repetition in this book, and that I say the same thing again and again. But it is difficult to change a whole way of thinking — and it is helpful to be reminded often.

There are many areas in which we may use our letters to express our views and to make suggestions or corrections. Some of the areas may concern the government (local, state, and national, which we have already mentioned). We should always feel free to write to our elected and appointed officials. Other areas may concern the media, charitable organizations, the schools — and you may think of many other areas in which your corrections and suggestions would be beneficial. Before you send a communication, however, you should make the effort to find the name of an individual who is in a position to respond to your correction or suggestion, and address the communication to their special attention.

Other Kinds of Letters

There are other kinds of letters that we should not neglect to write. They are letters of appreciation and gratitude. We most frequently focus our attention on areas that we feel need correcting or improving. And we forget how important it is to express our gratitude and appreciation to those whose actions and attitudes deserve to be recognized and acknowledged. Our letters provide an opportunity for us to let love (an experience of oneness) flow forth to bless the individual and to consciously release him or her into their Christhood or True Identity. And we, ourselves, are blessed by the act itself as the love and Spiritual Energy flow forth through us.

Don't Talk About It and Don't Try to "Help" People

There is something else that I want to mention. Don't talk about the forgiveness work to anyone. And for goodness sake, don't try to "help" somebody by telling them what they ought to do. Just be sure that you've done it yourself.

You see, if we think something is a great idea and we give away what we "think" it's all about — when we haven't even experienced it ourselves — we are just giving away words without meaning, and perhaps the wrong words or the wrong meaning. Thus, we not only dilute and dissipate the power of the idea itself — depriving ourselves of its benefit — but we are apt to misrepresent the message and the application it has to offer.

I am asking you not to speak of this work to anyone. Don't tell somebody that they ought to write down the name of everyone that they have ever condemned. Have you done it? And even if you have done it, don't tell anybody about it. You will lose it yourself, and those you are trying to "help" probably will think you are just "off your rocker." It is important to remember that the only thing we can give to another is the fruitage of our own consciousness. So let's give our attention to developing our own consciousness, and allow the fruitage to tell the story.

Let's get our own consciousness changed so that we develop a healing consciousness. And then when others come into our presence, they may say, "What is it that you have? Where did you get this? I see a change in you. I know that you have something." Let them ask. Then you can tell them where they can purchase a book or a recording.

I know that I used to want everybody to do what I did. Whatever it was that I had discovered and was reading or studying, I wanted everybody else to do it too. I'd buy up a bunch of books and give one to anybody who'd come into my orbit. And I always "worked on" — or tried to "work on" — my parents. I was an only child, and I was always trying to get my parents to do whatever I was doing.

But my Mother said to me, "We haven't seen that this has done so much for you. And when we do, we will ask you. Until that time, you just tend to your own business, and we'll tend to ours." When we think about the things we've done — trying to "work on" people, trying to "change" them, or trying to "help" them — it's really embarrassing, isn't it?

The Woman on the Subway

This reminds me of an experience I had. One time, I was on the subway, and a woman came through the subway car passing out cards that said, "Help the poor." She had a little box, and was taking up a collection. As I sat there, I was "working on" her. Then I thought, "This is the strangest thing. She has gone through the entire subway car and given one of those cards to everybody except me."

And I thought, "Well now, you see, she's getting this help that I'm giving her. She doesn't need to give me a card, because she's getting something else."

When she had finished giving out the cards and collecting the money, she came back and reached up and held onto the strap right above my head. She shook her finger in my face and said, "Everybody can't be so smart!"

Do you see what we do when we are "working on" someone in order to try to change them humanly, or to "help" them? We often feel proud of ourselves, because we think we are helping them "spiritually." But we are actually condemning them to their humanhood, and they "feel" it and resist and resent it. So it's much better

for us, and much better for the consciousness of
mankind for us to tend to our own business — which is
changing our own consciousness.

When We Feel That Condemnation
Really Is Justified

There are areas in our experience in which our condemnation may seem so totally justified that we don't think
of it as condemnation at all. We may dislike the kind of
work we are doing. We may detest the place where we
work. We may not get along with one or more of our
co-workers. We may feel that our boss is inconsiderate
and doesn't appreciate us. If we are the boss, we may be
irritated with an employee (or employees), or we may
be frustrated with our inability to satisfy a client. We
may be resentful because we don't even have a job at all.
We may hate the place where we live, or we may be
annoyed with our neighbors. We may be upset about
any number of situations in which we are involved.

We may be dissatisfied and angry and want to do
something different, or be some place else — just any
place else. We think everything would be great if only
something that we have a vague notion of would happen
to get us out of where we are. Whenever we have a
disgruntled "if only" attitude about where we are and what
we are doing, we are simply enveloped in condemnation.
And if we look deeply enough, we will find that we are
always blaming somebody else for our plight. It's always

somebody else's fault. When we allow ourselves to be consumed with condemnation — no matter how justified it may seem — we must realize that we are cutting ourselves off from the Source.

Have you ever found yourself so miserable and unhappy about a situation, a condition, or a place that you definitely decided to "make a change"? I can tell you this: It won't make very much difference if you go and put yourself someplace else. If you leave one situation or place because you "just can't take it any longer," you probably will find the same situation the next place you go. We always take ourselves with us.

Before we "move on," we must first lift up the situation or the place where we are. "The place whereon thou standest is holy ground." The original meaning of the word "stand" is upright. So that wherever we happen to be, we must stand upright in it. Then we can rise up out of a situation or a place — but we can't just walk away from it. We must first lift it up. You are in charge, and you have a responsibility. Wherever we are and whatever we are doing is our "ministry."

If I Lose My Job and Have to Look for Another One

Someone asked me, "What do you do about rejection when you are looking for a job?" I remembered a student who had lost his job and was desperate to find another one — and he asked me for help.

Of course, my theme is always forgiveness, non-condemnation, and non-judgment. The first thing I asked him to do was to recognize that he was bound to be feeling condemnation toward the one who had fired him, and maybe toward others as well. He would have to acknowledge all those he was condemning — or had condemned. And then the next thing for him to do was to use the steps of the Procedure for Forgiveness with each of the individuals.

We have to look for areas of condemnation and judgment and then forgive everyone who is involved in order to clear the way — and to "change the channel." As long as we remain tuned to the same channel, the experience will not change.

He did what I asked him to do. And then, when he began to look for a job, I told him to send love and forgiveness out ahead to those he would meet. So he followed my suggestions. And every time before he would go for an interview, he would call me from a phone on the street, and ask me to "be with him."

I asked him to be sure — when an interview was completed — that there was no condemnation or judgment, and that, as he departed, he was leaving a trail of love and forgiveness behind him. He continued this practice for several weeks with each of his many interviews. Suddenly — on the same day — he was offered three jobs.

He had become so involved with this new practice and experience that he almost regretted having it come to an end. And even though he was happy to have to choose one of the three jobs, he was going to miss "the ministry" he had just discovered. But, of course, he had also been preparing to carry this new level of consciousness into his new job. Since his consciousness had changed, the form and experience automatically changed. He had switched the dial to a different channel.

About Money and Giving

Now, I want to talk about money. It occurred to me that our attitude toward money represents us. We can learn a lot about ourselves if we observe how we feel about money. Money was always a problem for me.

When I began to teach piano, I taught children, and I charged six dollars a lesson. When a student stopped taking lessons, I would think, "Oh my goodness, this means I will have twenty-four dollars less income this month. Isn't this awful!" I began to realize that I was thinking of my students in terms of "six dollars" each time they came — and what a really terrible thing that was!

Then an idea came to me: "Instead of thinking in terms of what I am going to get from my pupils, I will tithe." So instead of writing down the "six dollars" that I was getting, I would write down "sixty cents" that I had to give. Ten percent was what I felt I could deal with at that time. And so as soon as a pupil left, I'd run in and write down "sixty cents." Another pupil would

come, and when they left, I'd write down "sixty cents."
Of course, I was turning my attention away from what
I was getting to what I could give. And this changed
everything for me. The arrows were now pointing
outward instead of inward. I was beginning to live
spiritually instead of humanly.

I realized that, until I began to "give," I had what we
sometimes think of as a "poverty complex." I was feeling
"poor" and scared, and I was depending on my pupils
to provide me with what I needed. I was looking outside
for "supply" to come to me. But when I started thinking
in terms of giving, my consciousness began to change.

We all live below the level of our potential consciousness when we live humanly — when we forget that
the Kingdom of Heaven is within us. The Spiritual
Energy of the Kingdom of Heaven is waiting to be
released as unconditioned form and experience — and
in ways that cannot be asked for, or prayed for, or even
imagined.

Before long, instead of teaching children, I began
teaching adults who had "always wanted to play the
piano." And since there was no material available for
teaching adults, I began to write my own material. Then,
instead of teaching the students individually, I began to
develop a method for teaching the students in groups.
And of course, since I could teach a lot more students,
my income increased so that I had more to give. The
"giving" turned everything around for me. And I soon
lost count of the proportion of what I could give.

We already know that the lack of forgiveness blocks us spiritually. But now we can see that the lack of giving also blocks us spiritually. The forgivingness and the givingness flow forth from within us. As we forgive and as we give, we are releasing the Spiritual Energy within us, which flows forth as unconditioned form and experience — "making all things new."

We don't "give" because we think we're going to "get" something back. We give because we feel an overwhelming urge to release The Infinite Invisible Spiritual Energy that is within us. We said earlier that our attitude toward money represents us. And so, as we give our money, we are acknowledging our oneness with All That Is. We are acknowledging our oneness with the Source within us and with our neighbor as ourself. Our giving is propelled by a sense of gratitude, which we release with the "act of givingness." It is not possible to describe — it must be experienced. And it becomes a new way to live.

Since the forgivingness and the givingness flow out from within us, we should ask ourselves: "Is there any-one that I am still holding in bondage — refusing to forgive?" If the answer is, "Yes," then I am blocking the flow of the Spiritual Energy from within me, and I am cutting myself off from the Source. "What have I to give? What can I give? What have I given? Am I hang-ing on to what I feel is mine? What am I willing to give? What have I in the house?" We should pour the drop that we have. It primes the pump, and the flow begins. And then we should observe whether we are continuing to let the Spiritual Energy pour forth in a steady flow.

In the Old Testament, there is an account of the Prophet Elijah asking the widow for a morsel of bread. The widow replied that she had only a handful of meal in a barrel and a few drops of oil in a cruse, which she expected to use to prepare food for her and her son to eat, and then to die. The Prophet told her not to be afraid, and to go and do as she had planned, but first to make him a cake and bring it to him. Then, she could make a cake for herself and her son. She acted according to Elijah's instructions, and "the barrel of meal wasted not and neither did the cruse of oil. And they ate for many days."

The preceding story always reminds me of the Bible passage in the Book of Proverbs which says: "Honor the Lord with thy substance, and with the first-fruits of all thine increase. So shall thy barns be filled with plenty, and thy presses shall burst out with new wine."

We can see that these examples illustrate the principle of givingness — the necessity of releasing the Infinite Invisible Spiritual Energy Within.

On one of Joel's tapes, there is a story that he told about a woman who had been asking him for help with a problem. He had been working with her for a long time, and the problem seemed not to yield. And on this particular day, Joel said to her, "You should give me something." The woman replied, "I don't have anything to give." Then Joel asked her, "How did you get here?"

The woman said, "I came on the street car." And Joel said, "Can't you give me that dime and walk home?" We can see now that Joel was giving the woman an opportunity to start the flow of Spiritual Energy — to open out a way for the imprisoned splendor to escape.

Giving of Ourselves in Service

There is another kind of giving — and it is the giving of ourselves in service to others. When we decide to give of ourselves in service to others, however, we should be sure that we do not allow ourselves to fit into the category of being a "do-gooder." Do-gooding is originated by personal sense, and it emphasizes and magnifies the sense of separateness. If personal sense decides that someone needs help, which it (personal sense — separate and apart) believes that it is capable of giving, the cause is lost before it begins.

Unless the act of service to others comes from within, and flows outward in an "experience of oneness," it is personal sense that is adding to itself and "puffing itself up." Before we "give of ourselves in service to others," we should ask whether we are "experiencing separateness," or whether we are "experiencing oneness." If there is an "experience of oneness," all are blessed.

We all can give some kind of service in an impersonal — and loving — way. I feel strongly about volunteer service. As a volunteer, I taught music once a week for eight years in a Veterans Hospital. Those whom I taught benefitted and were blessed by what they learned and from our "experience of oneness" — but I felt doubly blessed.

In our community, we can always find an opportunity to give a gift of service. When I first suggested this idea to the students, one of the men said, "I don't know what I could do." And I asked him, "What gift do you have within yourself that you could give or share — something that is special to you?" Then I remembered that he liked to hike, and I said, "Why don't you go to a Boys' Home and ask them to allow you to take some of the boys hiking with you each week?"

He followed through with the suggestion, and found that those in charge of a particular Boys' Home were delighted with the idea. And so, each week for several years, he would take some teenage boys, and some younger than teenage, hiking with him. They would walk along together in the quiet — sharing in the joy of the "experience of oneness." This activity became one of the rewards that the boys anticipated and enjoyed when they had "earned" the right to go. And for the student, it became "a ministry without words."

There are many things that each of us can do. We can give of ourselves in service through acts of kindness, compassion, and thoughtfulness to others. There are countless opportunities that are available for us to give of ourselves in a loving way. But, first of all, we have to give our thought, intention, and attention to the idea.

Trying to Establish Peace in the World From a Little Town in Texas

I didn't like going to college, and I wanted to get my degree as soon as possible. So I took extra courses during the school year and correspondence courses during the summer. And I graduated in three years. What I am going to tell you now took place during a summer vacation when I was at home from college.

It seemed to me that there was always a war going on someplace. I was very aware of the lack of peace in the world. And I thought how awful it was that countries couldn't get along.

Then I realized that in the little Texas town where we lived, there were seventeen churches, and people from one church hardly ever went to one of the other churches. And they never seemed to care about each other. This seemed like a representation of what was going on in the world — except that nobody was fighting. But it made me think a lot. And I tried to figure out some way of getting the churches in our little town to cooperate.

I had an idea that, for one month, we could have meetings that would include all the churches. On Wednesdays, for one month, all the churches could leave the doors unlocked so that people could go there and pray. And then, in the evening, we could have a meeting when everybody got together.

I spoke to a minister about it, but he didn't seem to respond too much to the idea. But then I presented my plan to another minister and he liked it, and said he would help me get it going.

I mentioned earlier that there were seventeen churches, but one of the churches didn't want to participate. There were sixteen churches, however, who agreed to be a part of the plan. I don't recall the names of all the churches, but there were Baptists, Methodists, Presbyterians, and others to add up to sixteen. This included the four churches that the black (African-American) people attended.

Since there were sixteen churches, and four Wednesdays in the month, four designated churches could participate in the meeting each week. And each group always included one of the churches attended by the black people. The minister, or the individual, who was representing each of the four participating churches, could either speak or say a prayer.

I got the fire department to blow the fire whistle briefly every morning at eleven o'clock throughout the month to remind everybody to be quiet for a moment and say a prayer for peace. There was an enormous amount of publicity in the local paper and on the radio.

The first big meeting was held at the Methodist Church, and I conducted the meeting. I don't recall the names of the churches that made up our group of four, but the individual who represented each group of the four churches gave an inspiring talk or prayed a beautiful prayer.

The second meeting was held in a black church. And of course, they shared the meeting with the other three designated participating churches. Lots and lots of people attended. I remember that cars were parked everywhere.

The meetings continued for two more weeks, and the interest and — I might add — the amazement mounted. But the month ended. And the town suddenly seemed quiet and sort of sad.

I see now that, at a relatively early age, I was already aware of the "separateness" among the churches. And I felt that the churches should be the ones to set the example for the world. Without recognizing it, I was attempting to bring about an "experience of oneness." I didn't really understand what I had undertaken, but I later realized that it had been a precursor of the work that I would ultimately attempt to bring forth to all mankind.

About Wars

One of the students asked, "How come there are wars? Why do we have them?" We will have wars as long as there is destruction in human consciousness. I probably should say, "As long as there is human consciousness" — because human consciousness is the sense of separation from God and from each other. And therefore everything is judged as an advantage or a threat. Wars are the magnified activity of personal sense. If something is an advantage, we want it, and we are willing to fight for it. If something is a threat, we want to get rid of it or destroy it. There will be wars as long as there is judgment, condemnation, and lack of forgiveness.

When we observe what goes on within us, we can see how we, ourselves, contribute to the wars in this world. Earlier, we spoke about the waveband that is made up of a composite of all the theories and superstitions that have arisen out of the belief of a separate selfhood — the sense of separation from God and from each other. We said that the waveband or frequency acts like a station on the radio that is constantly broadcasting.

If we accept these beliefs — or even one of them — or if we indulge in judgment, condemnation, or lack of forgiveness, we automatically adjust the dial so that we become vulnerable and subliminally susceptible to all that is being broadcast. As you know, we call this frequency the "universal mesmerism" or the "universal hypnotism" — and we are under its "spell."

But there is another aspect to all of this, that we may not realize. You see, our own thoughts, beliefs, judgments, condemnation, and refusal to forgive are not just confined to our own experience. And they do not disappear when we think or "feel" them. Every time we judge, condemn, or refuse to forgive, our thoughts —

reinforced by our emotions — float out and enter this waveband or frequency. And they stay there until they are canceled out by love (an experience of oneness). The startling phenomenon is that whatever we contribute to the waveband is available to all mankind.

Now, let's get back more specifically to wars. Of course, wars are fueled by hatred, greed, determination to dominate, and lack of forgiveness. When we see what we've done as individuals, it enables us to understand that those who are engaged in wars are doing just what we have been doing on another level. Now can we see that we must lift up those who are engaged in wars in the same way in which we've lifted up individuals in our own experience?

Wars are the ultimate in separateness. There are two sides, and those on each side condemn those on the other side and want their side to win.

We, ourselves, usually choose the side that we want to win, and we condemn and blame the opposing side. That which we are witnessing is the universal mesmerism functioning in those engaged in both sides of the war. We must realize that God constitutes the Being of each individual, and we must establish an experience of oneness. We do this by withdrawing our condemnation and blame from each individual on each side, and with love (an experience of oneness) allow the "I that I am" to release into his or her Christhood each individual who is involved.

Disasters of All Kinds

Disasters of all kinds — storms, tidal waves, floods, tornadoes, and all forms of destruction — are a part of the human consciousness to which we contribute by our own judgment, condemnation, and lack of forgiveness.

I realize that I have poured out enough condemnation to make a storm — to make a tornado. So wars, storms, and disasters of all kinds will continue as long as there is human consciousness.

I have to do my part to remove this destruction from the consciousness of mankind. I must cancel out or erase my own contribution to the waveband or frequency that we spoke of earlier. And the only way I can do it is by withdrawing judgment and condemnation of those in my own experience, and in my awareness, and by forgiving and releasing them into their True Identity. It is important to remember that when we are judging and condemning and refusing to forgive, we are contributing to the waveband or frequency that affects all mankind, and we are opening ourselves to all that exists in the human scene. On the other hand, when we cancel out our own contribution, we are canceling it out not only for ourselves, but for the consciousness of mankind as well.

Asking for Help

The subject of asking for help is rarely, if ever, discussed. This subject can easily be misinterpreted or misunderstood. But there is an important principle involved, and it concerns the completion of a circle.

When the individual or teacher who is asked for help gives what he or she has to give, and the student who is asking for the help gives what he or she has to give, the circle is complete. Otherwise, the student who is asking for the help is seeking something from the outside to come to him or her. This is living humanly. Therefore, whatever benefit the student receives from the contact is totally from the consciousness of the one who is giving the help.

Whereas, if the student lets something flow forth from within as gratitude and acknowledgment, he or she is living spiritually. Through giving, the student releases the Spiritual Energy from within, thus opening out a way — and the circle is completed.

Often, students say, "What do I owe you?" And I say, "You don't owe me anything. There is no fee, and you will not receive a bill. If you wish to send something, you may — but that is up to you." The responsibility must be left totally with the student. It is an opportunity for the student to release the Spiritual Energy from within himself or herself through the act of "giving" and expressing gratitude — rather than "paying for a service."

Sometimes students say, "I don't want to bother you." And I say, "It's not a matter of bothering me. If you are thinking of bothering me, you are thinking that I, personally, can give you help. And you are mistaken. The personal sense of I can't help you. But my consciousness — the 'I that I am,' at one with the Infinite Invisible Source — can help you." Often students call me on the phone and do not receive an answer. Although I may not be consciously aware that they called, if they are reaching out to my consciousness and not to me personally, they sometimes receive the help instantly.

When an individual is asking for help, it is important to be considerate, and to realize that it is not the same as "Dial a Prayer." I must say that I have been awakened many times in the middle of the night with requests such as, "Give me help, I can't sleep."

Another thing that students sometimes say is, "Would you give me a little bit of help?" This request says a lot. They are not really wanting to take the responsibility for asking in the first place. The request should be forthright and complete — with the recognition that they will take the responsibility for having asked.

When students say, "Would you give me a little bit of help?" I ask them, "Just how much help would you like?" And I sometimes tell them a story about myself. When I was a young child, we lived in a very small town. And my parents would buy the groceries and charge them during the week, and pay the bill on Saturday night. Each time they paid the bill, the grocer would give me some candy, or a gift of some kind. On this particular Saturday night, he gave me an apple, which I clutched with both hands — holding it tightly against my chest. And I stood there without saying a word. My Mother shook me by the shoulder and said, "What do you say?" And I said, "I want a sack-full." When I tell this story, the students never again ask for "a little bit of help."

When asking for help, the primary requisite is simply "to ask," but to ask whole-heartedly, with no reservations — accepting the responsibility for making the request. Many times, students will describe a problem, or hint that a situation needs attention. And even though they want help, and hope they will receive it, they just don't — and won't — ask. The Bible passage, "Ask, and ye shall receive" must also mean, "Ask, and open yourself — be receptive — and ye shall receive."

There was an incident that Joel and Emma told me about, which illustrates this point. They were going someplace in the car, and Emma said to Joel, "I have a terrible headache." Joel did not comment. After a while, she said, "My headache is getting worse." Joel still did not respond. The third time Emma said, "My headache is unbearable. Why don't you give me help?" And Joel said, "Why don't you ask?"

You may wonder how "to ask." That is, you may wonder what you should say when you want help. You may simply say, "Please give me help," or "Please keep me in your consciousness," or "I'm calling for a contact," or "Please be with me." Students often ask whether they should state what the problem is. If they wish, they may tell me — but it isn't necessary for me to know. I always make it clear that I am not a counselor. Therefore, no discussion of the problem or situation is necessary.

The request, however, should be brief. Here is an example: I received a call from an eight year old boy who said, "Please give me help with my behavior." That is as brief and direct as a request needs to be.

When we ask for help with a problem, just what is it all about? Who is asking? Is it the "I that I am" — at the Center of My Being? Or is it "me" — the personal sense of I, cut off from the Source — caught up in the hypnotism of the human scene? Can the human scene be fixed up? Of course it can't. But if it could be fixed up temporarily, another problem may quickly erupt — and almost always does. Therefore, do you see that it is not the problem that needs healing, but it is the sense of separation from God, the Source, that needs healing. And how is this done?

When a call comes for help, if I see that this is a person with a problem, there is no help available. The call comes to me as my temptation to judge by appearances. But if I see immediately that this is only an appearance, and that, even though the one who is calling for help may not know it, he or she is actually asking to be released from the sense of separation from the Source and reestablished in their Christhood or True Identity.

I cannot judge by appearances, but I must judge righteous judgment. The righteous judgment is: "God constitutes individual Being." And that means that God constitutes the Being of the one who is asking for help.

My conscious realization that, since God (Omni-presence, Omnipotence, Omniscience) constitutes the Being of the individual who is asking for help, the problem that is being presented has no power or life of its own. It is simply the universal mesmerism presenting itself to me as a problem. It is my temptation. And this realization is my assurance that there is nothing that I (the personal sense of I) can do about the request. Why is this? If God (Omnipresence, Omnipotence, Omniscience) constitutes My Being and the Being of the individual who is requesting the help, is there anything in the human scene to be dealt with?

The individual who has requested the help may or may not instantly experience a release from the problem. Or, the answer may not come in the form they were expecting. Or, he or she may call for continued help. But the kind of help that is given can enable the individual to experience a change of consciousness. And when consciousness changes, the form and experience change. Unless consciousness changes, however, one problem may be met, and another immediately arise to take its place. Many students call regularly only for the purpose of asking for help and support in changing their consciousness. It is understood, of course, that those who request the help are cultivating the soil of their own consciousness by studying and practicing — to the utmost of their ability — the principles that have been presented in this book.

Not everyone is receptive to this kind of help. And even though they would like to be "rid of" their problems, they may not care to risk a drastic, or even a mild, change in their consciousness at this time. Many prefer to talk about their troubles and to discuss their problems. I said earlier that I am not a counselor, and I do not give advice. Therefore, if they wish to receive help of that nature, they probably will find other methods to be more satisfactory.

Some may be embarrassed or too proud to ask for help. Others, for whatever reason, simply will not ask at all. They want to do it themselves — or they feel that they should. I recall that, in my early experience with The Infinite Way, I felt that I had to prove that I could do it all by myself. I see now that it was personal sense wanting to stay "in charge" — and not "let go." Finally, I asked Joel what else I could do, and he said, "You can keep in closer touch." And from then on, I did.

It was much later, however, that I realized that Joel was giving me a great opportunity by telling me to keep in "closer touch." It was difficult to recognize, at first, that it was not the person, Joel, but his Enlightened Consciousness that "lifted" my consciousness when I made the contact and asked for help. And of course, each time I made the contact and consciously became receptive, his realization of my True Identity "melted" more personal sense, thereby enabling my own consciousness to become more enlightened. We seldom understand this aspect of what we have come to call "asking for help."

Whether we are asking for help for the resolution of a problem, or for help in consciously realizing our oneness with the Source, our own consciousness changes. The problem may dissolve, but what is important is that which takes place in our own consciousness through the contact with an individual whose consciousness is enlightened. Even though we may call for a contact concerning a problem, the individual who is giving the help deals only with the Spiritual Nature of our Being — recognizing our Christhood or True Identity.

We may just want to fix things up a bit — like getting everything reupholstered. But we really aren't quite sure that we want to invest enough to go all the way and completely renovate our consciousness. We may even feel scared that this kind of an experience may change things more than we bargained for. Would you like to know why we feel scared? Do you know what it is that is scared? Take a guess! It is personal sense. And it is scared because it knows that if we go all the way, it won't be able to stick around. But what is it that has been having problems in the first place? Of course it is personal sense. Isn't personal sense the sense of separation from God — the sense of being cut off from the Source? So what is the answer? The answer is to consciously reestablish the awareness of our oneness with the Source, at the Center of Our Own Being.

The Sense of Separation

Do you realize that the secret of the dilemma of the human scene is the illusion, or the sense, of separation or apartness? Oneness is our true state of Being: Oneness with God, the Source; Oneness with our neighbor; and Oneness with All That Is. Nothing can change that. There is no separation or separateness or apartness. But we can *believe* that we are separate, and behave accordingly.

When we were discussing the Garden of Eden in the third chapter of Genesis, we found that the serpent is the most subtle of all the beasts.

You know that the word "serpent" means "separateness" or "apartness," and the word "subtle" means "difficult to detect and crafty." There is an "appearance" of separateness or apartness — but it is not so. It is only an appearance or an illusion — which is difficult to detect and crafty.

Later we found that the Lord God said to the serpent (the sense of separateness or apartness), "You are cursed above all cattle." The meaning of "cursed" is "calamitous and abominable misfortune." And the original meaning of the word "cattle" is "personal property" (that which we own). The Lord God was saying that the most "cursed" (calamitous and abominable misfortune) of all that we "own" (claim to be ours) is the belief of separateness or apartness. This means that the most cursed of all our possessions is "our belief that we are separate or apart from God (The Infinite Invisible Source at the Center of Our Very Own Being)."

Are we really hearing this? We say, "Isn't this amazing?" We can repeat the words. And although we acknowledge that this has been the secret underlying human existence, even a slight "glimpse" is such a radical and overwhelming revelation that we simply cannot "take it in."

We say that we can intellectually accept the fact that it is so. But we do not *realize* it! Do you observe that we say that we *intellectually* accept that it is so? And do you recall that the intellect does not comprehend the things of the Spirit? The intellect deals only with the outer. So what has happened? What is this all about? We have been asleep. "Awake thou that sleepest, and Christ will give thee light." Actually, the passage is, "Awake thou that sleepest, **arise from the dead**, and Christ will give thee light."

What does it mean, "Arise from the dead"? You will recall that in the Garden of Eden, the Lord God told them that if they ate of the tree of the knowledge of good and evil (that is, if they judged good and evil), they would surely die. And "to die" means "to be cut off." Of course, they ate of the tree and, obviously, they did die — they cut themselves off, or separated themselves from the Source. The belief of separateness or apartness from God (the Source) was accepted and acted upon as the Truth. And, therefore, we have remained cut off from the Source — or "dead" to who we really are.

Do we realize that we perpetuate the belief of separateness or apartness by condemnation, judgment, and the lack of forgiveness? Have you ever wondered why forgiveness, non-condemnation, and non-judgment are so important? If there is lack of forgiveness, there is a sense of separateness; if there is condemnation, there is a sense of separateness; if there is judgment, there is a sense of separateness.

But where there is forgiveness, there is an "experience of oneness"; where there is non-condemnation, there is an "experience of oneness"; and where there is non-judgment, there is an "experience of oneness." Of course, an "experience of oneness" is love. Now, we are prepared to accept more light on Jesus' admonition, "Love (have an experience of oneness with) the Lord thy God with all thy heart, with all thy soul, and with all thy mind; and love (have an experience of oneness with) thy neighbor as thyself."

We must now awaken from this sleep — arise from the dead — and reclaim our birthright. "Be still, and know that 'I' (at the Center of My Very Own Being) am God." The "I that I am" is at one with the Source; the "I that I am" is at one with my neighbor; the "I that I am" is at one with All That Is.

What We Should Know and Do By Now

If we have been following the suggestions presented in this book, we have begun to establish a new way to live. We should meditate, and we should study, and we should give of ourselves in service to others, as we let the Spiritual Energy of givingness flow steadily through us. And of course, we should work with the forgiveness lists — keeping alert and continuing to add to the lists daily. As you know, however, adding the names to the lists is not sufficient. We must follow the steps of the Procedure for Forgiveness with each individual whose name is on the list until we feel that we can check their name off — because we have established an "experience of oneness" with them.

But we should not be surprised if we find that, later, we need to place a particular name on the list again — and perhaps many more times. We know that Jesus said, "Forgive seventy times seven." Each time we place a name on the list, by all means we should go through the entire Procedure for Forgiveness. If we feel frustrated that the same name keeps coming back again and again, we should remember that we can be forgiven only as (in the degree that) we forgive others. And we certainly should know by now that Jesus said, "If *ye* would be the children of God, pray for your enemies."

Taking Piano Lessons and Teaching Others

Throughout the book, I have mentioned experiences concerning my own piano lessons, and my search and discovery of new ways of teaching others. This section of the book is a recapitulation and an expanded summary of my experiences.

I started taking piano lessons when I was about seven. My parents were not particularly musical. But

Mother sang in the church choir, and Daddy had a trombone. There was a gazebo-like band stand on the City Hall lawn, and Daddy played in the band when they occasionally gave a performance on a Saturday night. And he marched in a parade when there was one. But I don't remember that he ever had to practice.

I had to practice early in the morning before I went to school. I got bored quickly — practicing the exercises and pieces that I had to learn. And it seemed that I was always having to get ready to play in a recital, or a contest, or a music festival. I had a clock on the piano bench beside me — and I don't know how I ever got away with it — but sometimes I'd turn the clock ahead, and get to school before the janitor did.

One morning I was so bored that I "made up a piece." Mother was in the kitchen washing the dishes, and she called out, "What is that you are playing?" I said, "It's a new piece." She said, "When did you get it?" And I replied, "Last time." By then she was approaching through the dining room, drying a dish. She asked, "What is the name of it?" And I said, "Sunset." By this time, she was standing behind me, and she said, "Where is it?" I pointed to my music, and said, "Here." I was pointing to one of my exercise books. Although Mother didn't play the piano, she could read music, and obviously I was caught — as they say, "red-handed."

I sat there waiting to get the spanking of my life. But she didn't spank me. And I went to school almost wishing I'd received the punishment then and there, because all day long, I kept wondering what was coming when I got home.

She never did spank me. But she told my teacher, who gave me a lecture at my lesson the next day. My teacher said that I should never do that again. I should always practice the pieces and exercises I was supposed to practice — so that I could win the contest. That was all the punishment I needed. I despised those contests — but I always won.

Once, when I was in high school, I was out with some friends in a car, and someone slammed the car door on my finger. The pain was excruciating, but my first thought was, "I won't have to play in the contest this year!"

I was aware, however, that some enjoyed the competition — and the contests were no problem for them at all. But for me, performing had actually become identified with competition. And I felt deep inside that learning music was for a purpose other than winning a contest.

I have mentioned before that when I graduated from college, my teachers thought that my talent was so exceptional that I should consider a career as a performer. But I knew that I didn't want to become a concert pianist. Later, I realized that the contests — as I was growing up — had a profound influence on my feeling about not becoming a performer. I did know, however, that I wanted to teach. And so I did.

I might add here that when I began to teach, I taught children. But I wouldn't let my pupils play in the contests. The parents wanted their children to participate in the competitions, so I promptly lost all of my pupils. But then I found that almost every adult I met would say, "I've always wanted to play the piano." And so from then on, I taught only adults. Since there was no available material written for teaching adults, I wrote my own material.

I devised a totally new approach, which enabled me to teach large groups of students — using only one piano. I trained teachers who wished to use the method I had developed for teaching their own students individually and in groups. I taught in several universities and institutions. And as a volunteer, I taught in hospitals — teaching patients with mental and physical disabilities. Some of the patients were confined to their beds, and I taught them without using a piano.

Increasingly, I became aware of the value and importance of the study of music as I witnessed the benefits in the lives of those I taught. I knew, however, that only a relatively small number of people would or could go to a teacher to take piano lessons. But I knew that if they could study at home at their own pace, they would not be deprived of the opportunity to experience the benefits of a music education. And so, over a period of years, I taught fewer and fewer students as I wrote, tested, refined, and later published *The McClintock Piano Course: A New Experience in Learning* (eight volumes of text and three volumes of music, and the Keyboard Concealer and the Interval Keyblocks). The Course makes it possible for anyone without previous knowledge of music or the keyboard to teach themselves to read music and play the piano — and to play musically.

When I had published the Piano Course (201 lessons — with music and text), I felt assured that a way was provided for everyone to have a complete music education. The Piano Course now does my teaching for me, as others, throughout the world, use the Course to teach themselves. And since it no longer requires my attention, I am free to devote all of my time to the spiritual work.

Joel had been impatient with me because I insisted on writing the Piano Course, when he felt that I should be traveling and teaching The Infinite Way. But when he saw the Course, he said that he had not realized that it contained all the spiritual principles. He said, "It will provide spiritual growth as well as enlightenment and fulfillment for anyone who works with it."

Sometime later, I played and recorded a collection of eight of my piano improvisations, which I call "Reflections of the Soul." There were so many requests for the music, that I produced a CD and a cassette. A reproduction of one of my paintings appears on the covers of the recordings, and also on the cover of this book. The recordings are distributed around the world. Often when I receive a telephone call from as far away as Thailand or Australia, it is a thrill to hear "Reflections of the Soul" being played in the background.

How I Approach My Daily Activities

One of the students asked, "To what degree should we plan our lives?" I do not make inflexible plans. Each day is a new day. I simply do what is at hand to do. But there is something that I always do — and it certainly requires no planning. The first and most important part of each day concerns my being sure that there is no one I am holding in bondage to my judgment or condemnation. And then, I can consciously acknowledge my oneness with the Source (Omnipresence, Omnipotence, Omniscience).

This is my assurance that the personal sense of I is not blocking the way for the Spirit to come through and do Its work. During the day, however, it is necessary for me to maintain a conscious awareness of my connection with the Source through my "mini-meditations," and with longer periods of "Being Still." And of course, I must constantly monitor myself and cancel out any judgment, condemnation, or lack of forgiveness.

The quality of the work that I am doing is affected by whether or not I stay focused in the present and remain open for inspiration. The inspiration does not come while my attention is focused "horizontally" — out ahead. The inspiration comes only when my attention is centered in the perpendicular split second of "the Now."

If a situation arises that requires me to make a decision or to take some action, I often ponder the situation and wait for direction. I do not find it profitable, however, to carry around the weight of indecision and let it "take up space." So I ask myself, "Is there anyone — anywhere — that I have not forgiven, or is there anyone I am holding in judgment or condemnation?" When I am sure that personal sense is not blocking the flow, I keep flexible, and proceed to do what is at hand to do.

If I have an obligation to meet concerning filling orders, paying bills, answering mail, or some aspect of my spiritual work, I feel that it is important to be con-siderate of others who may be involved. And therefore, I proceed without delay.

I have spoken about the "weight of indecision" taking up space. I find that indecision is akin to procrastination. How often do we procrastinate, and at the same time excuse ourselves by looking for someone or something to blame for keeping us from doing what we know we "should do" or "should have done"? "Doing what is at hand to do" releases me from the stagnant state of indecision and allows me to stay in "the Now."

When I begin to work on a project, it is revealing to observe the ingredients I have put "into the mix." Is there resentment and condemnation, or is there enthusiasm and joy? An experience of oneness is the secret — experiencing oneness with the activity itself as well as with all those who may be involved.

A wonderful example of experiencing oneness with the activity we perform is the following observation I made when I had my kitchen painted, not long ago. The painter carefully prepared the kitchen so that he would not spill a drop of paint, and after doing a beautiful and artistic job, he swept up every particle of dried plaster and paint, and left the kitchen spotlessly clean.

When I expressed my appreciation to him, he stood there smiling — his face covered with perspiration and paint — and he said, from the depth of his soul, "I *love* my work."

Ordinary Every-Day Condemnation and Judgment

When we find that we need to forgive, it is pretty obvious, and we know what we have to do. But ordinary every-day condemnation and judgment may slip by undetected. And we may consider that what we are condemning or judging is not the kind of thing that really counts. But it does.

Recently, I was walking down the street, and I saw a man that I caught myself judging. I was judging the way he was dressed and the way he was behaving. His behavior was not directed at me, and he was not even aware of me at all. Nevertheless, I was judging him. Suddenly, I actually heard these words spoken within me, "It's not worth it." The judgment stopped immediately. And I was able to acknowledge that "God constitutes individual Being," and therefore God constitutes the

Being of this individual. There was an instant "experience of oneness."

The words, "It's not worth it" made a profound impression on me. Later, I began to ponder the depth of their meaning. One idea was that it costs too much to judge — it's too expensive. Then it occurred to me that the price I am paying for judging and condemning is "cutting myself off from the Source." Is it worth it? "Cutting ourselves off from the Source" is the price we pay for our indulgence in judgment and condemnation.

Condemnation and judgment are decoys that keep us perpetuating the belief in separateness or apartness. This is why we have to be extremely vigilant. I find it revealing — and shocking — to observe how many times a day I can catch myself condemning and judging. And each time I catch myself, the words, "It's not worth it" come up immediately. And "oneness" is always waiting to be "experienced."

About Jealousy

One of the students asked me, "Is jealousy condemning?" My reply was, "If you are jealous of someone, are you experiencing oneness? Of course not. You are experiencing separateness. And you are condemning them *for* something and *to* a state of consciousness."

Jealousy is an insidious and pervasive emotion. It is like a smokescreen, which influences, alters, and distorts our attitudes and thoughts. And if we are accused of being jealous, we may deny it, and react with indignation and anger. We cannot tolerate having the word jealousy associated with us, and therefore, if we are jealous, we may refuse to admit it.

The victim of our jealousy is a silent and subtle enemy whom we condemn because we consider them to be a threat or a rival. They are preventing us from having something or someone that we want for ourselves.

We should place the name of the individual on our list and work with the steps of the Procedure for Forgiveness until we have established an experience of oneness.

About Secrecy

When we have a revelation that seems of great importance to us, we usually want to rush out and tell everybody about it. It is the hardest thing in the world to keep from talking about it. But when we find that we want to tell others about our discovery, we should look closely and observe whether we may be feeling proud of ourselves, and wanting to let others know about our "advanced" spiritual state. Telling others about it simply adds to personal sense.

It is difficult to accept the fact that secrecy is such an important aspect of our spiritual growth. That which has been revealed to us is from the Spirit. But the tendency is to want to bring this "spiritual treasure" into the intellect and put it into words so that we can talk about it with others. Whatever has touched us deeply enough for us to recognize that it is of great value has come to us from the Source. It is given to us to feed us spiritually, and thus change our consciousness. It is sacred, and it must be recognized as the "treasure" that it is, and kept secret.

If we have a revelation, or if we receive some light and then bring it into the intellect and put it into words so that we can tell someone about it, we will lose it. It's as if a seed has been planted, and before it even begins to sprout, we dig it up and give it to somebody. We can't do that without losing it. We should never talk about it until we have fruitage. We can give away our fruit, but we can't give away our seeds, our sprouts, our plants, or our blossoms. When it becomes fruit, and we know that it's bearing rich fruit, then we can begin to give it away.

You may say, "Isn't that being selfish?" No, it is not being selfish. We can't help another until we are witnessing the fruitage in our own experience. Do you know where that fruitage comes from? It comes from our own consciousness. And that is all we can give to another. Nothing else is of value. The words won't do it. Unless the words that we speak come from our consciousness (that is, our own experience of what we are saying), they not only are of no value to another, they may be totally rejected. And after we have talked about it, we often wonder what it was that we were so excited about anyway. It all seems so empty. We will have lost our "treasure."

We said earlier that, lots of times, those whom we are determined to help, don't even want it. They may feel that we're just "being smart." Or, as Mother said to me, "We don't see that this has done so much for you!" We have to be particularly careful, because the moment we begin to talk about some revelation we have had, or give "spiritual advice," we are going to be watched very closely.

We may say, "But I just want to share it with those on this Path." Don't do it! Do you recall that Jesus said, "Go show the priests, but don't tell anyone else." When students who are in very close touch with me have a deep spiritual experience, I say to them, "Don't tell me about it. Let it feed you. Don't speak about it to anybody — not even to me. Later, maybe you will want to tell me about it, but not until you can see that there is fruitage."

You will find that if you place your "treasure" in the mind and leave it there — keeping it sacred and secret — the Spirit can feed you in a way in which you've never been fed before. This is how consciousness changes. And then the pure unconditioned consciousness can flow forth and form fruit. Do you now see that it is only personal sense, wishing to add to itself, that would want to speak of such a sacred experience? Can you hear yourself say, "I had this revelation, and I'm going to tell you about it."? Then you've lost it.

We have been discussing the importance of refraining from telling others about our revelations or spiritual discoveries, but there is another — perhaps more important — aspect of the sacredness and secrecy that we may not be aware of. And it is this: When the Spirit ignites a message within us, we not only should not bring it into the intellect and put it into words and talk to others about it — we should not "talk to ourselves" about it either. If we discover that we are "talking to ourselves" about it, we can be assured that it is personal sense feeling proud and trying to add to itself. Personal sense is even apt to attempt to use it as a formula — which is a guarantee that the message the Spirit has given us will be lost.

An illustration that I often use in relation to secrecy and sacredness concerns the Christ child. At the time of Jesus' birth, Herod was the king, and he had received word that Jesus had been born. In his effort to destroy the Christ child, he issued an edict decreeing that all children two years of age and younger should be killed. To protect the Christ child, He was taken down into Egypt, where He could be hidden and kept secret until He was no longer in danger, and until He grew strong. Otherwise, He would have been killed.

This is an example of how we should protect a gift that we receive from the Spirit — a "spiritual treasure" — which we must not expose or allow to be destroyed. We must "take it down into Egypt" and hide it from the Herod of our own intellectualizing, analyzing, and personalizing. Our "spiritual treasure" must be protected and kept sacred and secret while we allow it to become strong, and to feed us, and to teach us, and to change our consciousness.

The principle of secrecy also applies to creative ideas that come to us concerning a new project or work that we may feel we wish to pursue.

When we have a new and exciting idea, we may be so elated that we want to tell everybody about it. And if we do, we will dissipate the power and the energy that accompanied the idea when it presented itself to us. The power and energy of the idea were for the purpose of propelling it toward fruition.

We should regard the idea as sacred, and "take it down into Egypt," and keep it hidden until it is strong and well enough established in our own consciousness for us to allow the energy of the idea to carry it to completion. Otherwise, later, we may wonder why nothing ever became of our "brilliant idea."

The Manna Flows Fresh Daily

There is something else I should say about having a revelation or a mystical experience. You may have such an experience, and you may or may not tell anyone about it. But it lifts you up, and you feel that a healing has taken place. And then after a while the experience fades — and you wonder where it went. You may say, "I know what happened, but it doesn't even make sense any more." You feel bereft because you thought you really had found the "answer."

Let it go. Don't try to recall it. Don't try to bring it back. The manna flows fresh daily, moment by moment.

So if it never happens again in the same way, don't be disturbed — just know that it is Infinite. The Spiritual Energy can manifest in many ways. Or you may simply experience the Silence. What a great gift that is! Or, maybe nothing seems to happen at all. You may be looking in a particular direction and expecting the Spirit to come and fill your concept of what you are seeking. And if it doesn't come that way, you think nothing has happened. Just remember: The manna flows fresh daily. Be still! "In the moment that you *think not*, the bridegroom cometh."

Joel said that many have had a mystical experience, and later felt that they had lost it. Then, they spent the rest of their lives trying to get it back again. It doesn't work that way. The Spirit is Infinite. So, why should we limit It to our idea of the way It should present Itself?

I have never allowed students to take notes in my music classes or in any other classes that I've taught. Because, when they are copying something or trying to "hold on to" something, they are functioning on the level of the intellect. Therefore, what they are "getting" is mere information, and they are missing the "experience." The Spirit is in "the experience" — not in the words they are trying to write in a notebook.

You may have notebooks and notebooks full of words you've written down in classes and at lectures. I have lots of them, myself, and I could rarely find a thing I was looking for — in case I ever did want to refer to what I had written. And if I did find what I was looking for, it didn't mean a thing. But if, instead of trying to write it down, we let "the experience" go straight into our consciousness, it will be ours. And when we need to know something, it will come back to us.

When something such as this message comes forth, either as I'm giving a class or as I am writing this book, it is the Spirit that is bringing it forth. It is really not the words that I speak or write, but it is the rhythm or the Spiritual Energy that you are feeling, as It is flowing straight from my consciousness into your consciousness — by-passing your intellect. The rhythm, or the Spiritual Energy, of the message flows forth, and the words that you hear or read form themselves around it.

A great teacher — a mystic — with whom I studied improvisation, once said something to me about rhythm that has remained one of my most sacred treasures. I now share it with you: "The rhythm, or the life current, of a plant goes up ahead of it, and the plant forms itself around it."

Missing the Point

When I gave classes here in New York, there were many students whose husbands or wives did not attend the classes and were not interested in the work at all. If I scheduled a class that a student wished to attend, but the timing interfered with an important date like a birthday, or a graduation, or some special activity for the family, I always said, "By all means, consider your family first. Your place is with your family. Never even think of coming to the class. And if they want to go to church, go to church with them."

One of the students had a wife and three children. His wife attended a church in the town where they lived, and although she was not interested in this work, she did not discourage him in any way. However, when he was ready to study or meditate, he wanted everybody to be quiet and not disturb him. I said, "For heaven's sake, don't make such an issue of it. Since your family are not interested, just do your studying and meditating when it does not interfere with any of their activities. Or find other opportunities to study and meditate. Are you aware of the condemnation you are heaping upon your wife and children, simply because you think they are not allowing you to be as spiritual as you think you want to be?"

Once I scheduled a class that he particularly wanted to attend. But it was on a weekend when there was a special event that his wife wanted him to attend with her. He was upset and resented the fact that he would have to miss the class. And he asked me what he should do about it. He already knew what my answer would be.

Then I added, "How do you think you would feel if you had to stay home with the three children all the time? Has it ever occurred to you to say to your wife that you would be glad to stay home with the children some Saturday and let her go to New York to the theater? Just try it and see what happens." So he tried it. At first she said, "Oh no, that's all right, I won't go." But finally she decided she would go. And he said, "Go ahead. Get yourself a new outfit to wear, and go to the theater." She decided she'd go to a poetry reading. She got a new dress and went to New York for the whole day — which was a rare treat. And which, incidentally, changed their entire relationship.

My Own Experience of "Missing the Point"

You can see that often in our attempt to be so "spiritual," we miss the point altogether. I realize that, for many years, I missed the point with my Mother. You already know that we had a rather rocky relationship. I always found it very difficult to leave her alone and let her be who she was, and not keep trying to change her and get her to do what I wanted her to do — which, of course, was to be as "spiritual" as I thought I was.

Now, however, I know that my soul chose my very special parents to help me experience every aspect of my life that has been necessary for my spiritual growth and development. There were glimmers along the way when I saw clearly the significance of particular experiences.

For example, I mentioned earlier about my taking flying lessons and about the reaction of my parents when they found out about it. And I also spoke about their opposition and resistance when I told them I was going to write the Piano Course. You may recall that at the time, I was writing a letter to God every morning, and I said to God, "Why can't Mother and Daddy understand that I just have to do this? If only they wouldn't resist what I'm doing! I know I have to do it!" And the answer came, "Their resistance is providing exactly what you need. After all, in order to rise, an airplane takes off into the wind."

I always wondered why there never seemed to be any possibility of our "getting along." And once, I spoke to a Swedenborgian minister about my concern and my wish to understand "why." He said, "Your parents thought they were having a chicken. They had a bird!"

I really did try to work things out, but — seemingly to no avail. When I came to New York to live, and would be preparing to go to Texas for a visit, I would pray, and deny, and affirm, and do all the things I knew to do, hoping and actually expecting to have that particular visit be the one that would bring us together. But when my parents would meet me at the airport, and we would be waiting for my luggage to come off the plane, a major disagreement would ensue. And we would engage in what is called, in Texas terms, "a knock-down drag-out." I always emerged dismayed, discouraged, disappointed, and perplexed that my efforts and intentions had failed again.

Our relationship was extremely difficult for me. But I realize how much suffering my parents endured as I stubbornly refused to do other than I felt impelled to do. Now, my understanding of how difficult the relationship was for my parents increases my appreciation for every "friction" that we experienced.

From the time I began the forgiveness work, my parents always headed my list, and I followed the steps of the Procedure for Forgiveness all the way. By this time, I knew, however, that what I was doing was for myself — not to change them.

During the last few years of my Mother's life, I had an even deeper desire to find a way to resolve our relationship. And finally, I was able to see clearly that the only solution was that I simply express love to her on a level that she could accept and understand. It is a joy to know that this was accomplished.

And she responded with the kind of love that I could accept and understand — including her acknowledgment of the importance of the Piano Course, and her encouragement for me to continue to write.

Although she was never in total agreement with my "spiritual work and activities," she tried. And once when I visited her in Texas, she asked me to make a recording of my reading some chapters from one of Joel's books, so she could listen to the recording when I returned to New York.

Today, I recognize and revere the integrity of my parents as I pour out gratitude and love for the great gift they gave me.

A Spiritual Challenge

What I am going to tell you now may not be what you would especially like to hear. But it is important for us all to be aware of.

When we feel committed to a spiritual path, we think that everything will turn out to be grand and glorious. We think that we will have health, prosperity, companionship, and all the benefits that we believe this world has to offer us as the "added things." Often there is improvement and change, and we do have a surge of better health, more supply, and perhaps the one we consider to be the ideal companion. But we shouldn't be surprised if things don't always turn out that way.

Even though we have committed ourselves to deepening our consciousness, we may find that we have an unexpected challenge to meet. I had such an experience not too long after I became dedicated to The Infinite Way. I feel that I should tell you about it, because those whom I have told have found it helpful. I had a very serious and severe health problem, which, I was told, required an operation.

We just didn't go to doctors on a regular basis when I was growing up. But I suppose I should back up to the beginning. When I was born, my throat was not developed sufficiently for me to breathe adequately. Nothing the doctors in the hospital tried would work, and they told my parents that since I couldn't possibly live, they should just take me home to die. So my parents took me home. There is no scientific explanation for why I didn't die — or why I lived.

When I was very little, they "took out" my tonsils. I recall being in the hospital, but I don't remember anything about the doctor, except that I was afraid of him. My main recollection of the experience is of my new pink bathrobe with kittens and balloons on it, which I had been given especially for the occasion.

Another experience we had with doctors was when I was in elementary school, and my father had to have an operation on his eye. He was so allergic to the medication that an inflammation developed to such an extent that he lost the sight of his eye. And later the same thing happened when he had an operation on his other eye. He was totally blind for a long time. And of course, I blamed the doctors. But sometime later he had other operations, which restored some of his vision.

Then, several years after that, Mother had to have an operation to remove her appendix. And I recall feeling that her having to have the operation just meant the end. I was always scared of doctors — particularly surgeons. And I was full of condemnation for them.

Now, I'll continue with the story I started to tell about finding out that I would have to have an operation. In addition to condemning doctors, I had adopted the attitude prevalent among those who were involved in metaphysical and spiritual studies. And that was that you just have to meet the problem spiritually. No allowance was made for the medical profession — whatsoever!

I asked Joel for help, but I wasn't able to receive it. I felt that it was such a spiritual disgrace to have to have an operation, that I would have preferred to just go ahead and die. But finally — completely overcome with fear and embarrassment — I agreed to have the operation.

The warmth and caring that was expressed by everyone I encountered in the hospital was beyond anything I could have imagined. The dedicated concern of the surgeon — prior to the operation, and when he greeted me as they wheeled me into the operating room — gave me all the assurance I could possibly have been able to accept at the time.

After the operation was over, and I was in my hospital bed in my room, I was so consumed with fear again that I was unable to control my emotions or thoughts. But the words: "God Is Now" came to me, and I said one, two, or three of those words over and over — day and night. Because any one, or any combination, of the words would bring me back into the split second of "the Now" — and keep me from dwelling on the past, or worrying out ahead about the future. I still use these three words, individually, or in any combination as mini-meditations. I had with me a little booklet of Joel's, called *The Deep Silence of My Peace,* which I read again and again and again.

Joel wrote me while I was in the hospital, and he said. "It will be very interesting to see what happens now." And I thought, "What a thing for him to say!"

Later, I often remarked that, in a peculiar way, the experience didn't seem to touch me. What I meant, of course, was that even though I didn't know how to express it at the time, the experience didn't touch the "I that I am."

After I came home from the hospital, I had to report to the surgeon's office for a check up. During the appointment, he made the most dire prediction imaginable about my future. When I questioned him, he said, "Well, I know what I had to do to you." It sounded as if I probably should not count on being around too much longer!

This amounted to total devastation — and I left his office reeling with fear. I got in a cab to come home, and a Voice very clearly spoke to me, saying, "Who is your authority?"

I knew that the doctor had spoken from the depth of his integrity, and I knew that he had performed the operation with utmost care and expertise. But I never returned to his office. And I've never seen him again.

When I had the operation, I had not yet had the revelation about what we do to ourselves by our condemnation, judgment, and lack of forgiveness. Now, however, I certainly do realize how thoroughly I condemned and judged doctors, and how afraid I was of them. Being freed of my condemnation and judgment of doctors was a necessary preparation for the spiritual work I was led to do.

I now understand that our soul chooses the challenges we need to meet for our spiritual growth.

I continued my spiritual studies. And within eighteen months I was in what is called the "healing work." That is, many began to call me for spiritual help — and still do. Later, Joel said to me, "I told you that it would be interesting to see what happened!"

The Crusader

I must tell you that I learned the hard way about the Biblical admonition to "not scatter our pearls before swine." This is such a drastic statement, and I was always offended by the word "swine." But now I understand that the word is actually referring to the "unprepared consciousness." That which follows is an account of how I learned my lesson.

I have told you about the revelation I had more than thirty years ago concerning the importance of forgiveness. At that time, the word "forgiveness" was not even commonly used, let alone a part of the general experience of the world. I was bewildered by all that was being revealed to me, and I kept it sacred and secret, not because of a spiritual principle, but because I thought people would think I was "strange." Then I finally got the courage to present the "idea of forgiveness" to the students at a weekly Infinite Way Tape Meeting that I was conducting. The students were not all responsive, but I tenaciously forged ahead anyway.

Meanwhile, I was involved in the activities of the New York City Opera Guild, which I had co-founded. The Infinite Way mail and the calls for help were increasing daily. I was continuing to work on the Piano Course, but I felt uncomfortable because Joel just didn't seem to understand how important the Piano Course was. I knew that he wanted me to travel around the world and give Infinite Way classes. Soon I began to give classes here in New York on the subject of forgiveness. The classes were attended not only by the local students but also by "unsuspecting" students who came from other areas as well. And I was shocked and dismayed at some of the belligerent letters I received from many who I thought would understand and embrace the message. But I was not deterred, because I felt that this message was the answer, and that it could "save the world."

Then, at Joel's urging, I gave classes not only here in New York but in other cities in the United States and Canada. I found that only a very small percentage of the students were ready to hear or to work with the message I was giving. Although it was "hard going," and I received great opposition, I had become such a crusader that it took me quite a while to "catch on" to what was happening, and so I continued to persist.

Finally, however, I realized that I was making a big mistake. I would have to "give up" and work only with those who were drawn to my consciousness, and who knew ahead of time the kind of message they were going to receive when they came to my classes.

So, from then on, I gave classes only in my own apartment. Students came from all over to attend the classes, but they knew what they were going to get, and they were ready for it. I asked the students not to speak of the message, but to work with it, and to keep it sacred and secret, so that it could "take root" in their own consciousness. They used the methodology for forgiveness that had been revealed to me, and they practiced the principles, which are now presented in this book.

I told the students that the only way that forgiveness could enter the consciousness of mankind was through our practicing the principles of forgiveness ourselves, and by developing our own consciousness. I made it clear that, although it might seem like a good idea to talk about it to others — and that they might feel that they would be helping someone by telling them what to do — they not only would lose it themselves, but they very likely would actually offend the ones they were trying to help. Furthermore, they would dilute and dissipate the message. We had to keep it sacred and secret until we were seeing rich fruitage in our own lives.

Those pioneering and dedicated students have kept in close touch with me all these years as they have continued to work, faithfully practicing the principles of forgiveness. I thank them and honor them for their part in helping to bring this message of forgiveness into the consciousness of mankind.

In 1993, I felt that it was time to release the recordings of a class I had given, called, *Love Greets You: Love, Forgiveness, Mind, and the Garden of Eden.*

These recordings are now being studied by hundreds of students throughout the world.

Since the recordings were released, I have sent invitations to the students who have purchased them, specifying particular weekends on which all of us, in our own homes, would join together in consciousness, and work with the recordings and practice the suggested procedure. The activity provides a Workshop for each student; and I take into my consciousness those who request to be included. The schedule (New York time) is indicated, and those in countries such as Australia and Thailand get up in the middle of the night to participate in the work. The students have found the Workshops to be a transforming experience. And because of their requests, I have scheduled the activity twice a year. We now have the Workshops in the Spring and in the Fall.

Almost every week, students send me articles concerning forgiveness that they have found in various publications, and they mention programs they have heard on the radio or seen on television. It is obvious that the *word* "forgiveness" and the idea of forgiving are entering human consciousness. But *how* to really forgive is another matter.

This book embodies and expands the work that is presented on the recordings. Neither supplants the other. And now that this book as well as the recordings are available, all of those who work with the suggestions and the procedures as they are presented will be a part of bringing this message, *Love and Forgiveness: A New Way to Live,* into the consciousness of mankind.

---------- Epilogue ----------

The Little Boy and His Dog: The True Prayer of Forgiveness

There is a poignant story that Joel told about a little boy whose dog was run over by a car and killed. Of course the child was devastated. His mother placed the body of the dog in a room to await the father's return home from work, so they could make the decision about burying the dog.

The little boy went into the room where the mother had placed the body of the dog, and he closed the door behind him. He stayed an inordinate amount of time — long after the father had returned home from work.

Suddenly, the door opened and the dog came running out. The parents couldn't believe what they were witnessing. They asked the little boy how he had prayed for his dog. And he replied, "I didn't pray for my dog, I prayed for the man who ran over him. Because I know how bad he must have felt."